MW00808075

WALKING ON WATER

Skeptics and Believers Discuss Whether Jesus Matters

Anita E. Keire

CURRICULUM DEVELOPMENT ASSOCIATES, INC

Curriculum Development Associates, Inc.
Greenwich, CT 06830-3027
www.mustardseedseries.com

ISBN: 099808770X
ISBN 13: 9780998087702
Library of Congress Control Number:2016915898
Curriculum Development Associates, Incorporated,
Greenwich, CT

Library of Congress Cataloging-in-Publication Data

Keire, Anita E.
Religion/Rudiments of the Christian Faith
John the Baptist
Jesus' Incarnation and Ministry
Coming to Terms with Jesus' Parables and Miracles
Divergent Thoughts on Forgiveness
Crucifixion and Resurrection of Jesus
The Emerging Christian Church to 80 CE
First Century Christian Religious History
Spirituality/Faith Development

Cover Photo: Leslie Mueller Design
Cover Design: Kia Heavey

God be in my head and in my understanding;
God be in my eyes and in my looking;
God be in my mouth and in my speaking;
God be in my heart and in my thinking;
God be at my end and at my departing.

Sarum Primer, 16th

Also by Anita E. Keire

Resurrection Dialogues with Skeptics and Believers
A Parent's Guide to Prayer
Mustard Seed Series Director's Book
Mustard Seed Series Teacher's Training Manual
Mustard Seed Series Kindergarten Teacher Book
Mustard Seed Series Kindergarten Student Book
Mustard Seed Series Primary 1 Teacher Book
Mustard Seed Series Primary 1 Student Book
Mustard Seed Series Primary 2 Teacher Book
Mustard Seed Series Primary 2 Student Book
Mustard Seed Series Intermediate 1 Teacher Book
Mustard Seed Series Intermediate 1 Student Book
Mustard Seed Series Intermediate 2 Teacher Book
Mustard Seed Series Intermediate 2 Student Book
Mustard Seed Series Junior 1 Teacher Book
Mustard Seed Series Junior 1 Student Book
Mustard Seed Series Junior 2 Teacher Book
Mustard Seed Series Junior 2 Student Book
Mustard Seed Series Pre-Confirmation 1 Teacher Book
Mustard Seed Series Pre-Confirmation 1 Student Book
Mustard Seed Series Pre-Confirmation 2 Teacher Book
Mustard Seed Series Pre-Confirmation 2 Student Book
Mustard Seed Series Confirmation Teacher Book
Mustard Seed Series Confirmation Student Book

Acknowledgements

I owe a debt of gratitude to some 20 well-educated people of divergent religious backgrounds who shared their thoughts, doubts, and beliefs with each other and me in a monthly three-year discussion group that I facilitated.

Many thanks also go to the Letters Women of the Greenwich, CT, Branch of the National League of American Pen Women who critiqued and offered helpful advice and encouragement in the creation of *Walking on Water: Skeptics and Believers Discuss Whether Jesus Matters.*

Walking on Water
Skeptics and Believers
Discuss Whether Jesus Matters

Table of Contents

Introduction

Walking on Water: Skeptics and Believers Discuss Whether Jesus Matters is the second book in my Mustard Seed Series Trilogy of the Christian story. My first book, *Resurrection Dialogues with Skeptics and Believers,* examines dominant Jewish and Christian beliefs on resurrection from antiquity to the present day. It also covers Liberal, Conservative, Neo-orthodox, and Postmodern religious views.

My current book examines the significance of Mary, John the Baptist, Jesus, and Paul. It examines the shape, meaning, and purpose of Jesus' ministry especially revealed to us through his teachings, miracles, parables, actions, suffering, forgiveness, death and resurrection. *Walking on Water* concludes with the emerging church and the spread of Christianity in the first century.

The third book in this trilogy to be published in late 2017 or early 2018 will cover the development of Trinitarian and Atonement theology and doctrine.

My purpose in writing these books is to help seekers, believers, and novices learn the rudiments of the Christian story. The dialogue continues with six characters whom you may have met in *Resurrection Dialogues.* Other than for myself, these characters are imaginative composite characters I created to represent major theological positions and their critics that exist within Christianity and Judaism. I will have them reintroduce themselves which they initially did in *Resurrection Dialogues.*

***

My name is **Mary**. I consider myself a faithful Roman Catholic. I went to Catholic schools all the way through college. I attend Mass every Sunday and on holy days. But the scandals within the church and their cover-ups have thrown me and other Catholics into spiritual and emotional turmoil. My own priest stole peoples' hard-earned money to support his partner in a New York City apartment. I wonder whether vows of priestly celibacy and poverty are all one big joke and hypocrisy. I go to different Catholic churches now but still feel alienated. I love mass and receiving Holy Communion. They are important to my spiritual life. My Catholic friends and I feel betrayed and are at a loss where to turn or what to do. We hope that Pope Francis will restore our trust in the church and in our priests and bishops. I hope he will lead and help us develop and sanctify our spiritual lives. In the meantime, I want to get a broader vision of Christianity and learn what I can from all of you.

My name is **Edward**. I am a physicist and come from a Protestant liberal family. I know science and religion have always sought peoples' acceptance for either one of these two positions. I choose not to belong to either camp. Mary's current state and misgivings with her church similarly caused me to reject authoritarian and all-knowing religions that claim for themselves to represent "God's word" and "God's law." Nor can I accept the idea that outside the church there is no salvation and that the church is the fount and boundary for all learning. An historical example of this hypocrisy is Galileo's scientific defense of Copernicus' findings that the earth is not the center of the universe. Because Galileo's scientific observations were not in accord with church teachings, the Inquisition unsuccessfully tried to make Galileo recant his position and forced him to live under house arrest until his death. Even then, the church denied him his final resting place. Like Galileo, I am a Christian believer, but find some of the movement in the churches to be too authoritarian or contrived and revisionist. Maybe our discussions can help me in my faith journey.

My name is **Sarah**. I am a Jew. I have raised my fist numerous times at God for allowing the persecution, discrimination, and hatred of the Jews. I ask myself what individual and collective responsibility Christians have in this treatment. Most of my family was killed during the Holocaust or Shoal. Fortunately for my immediate family and me, my father was teaching at Harvard University during that time. I feel we Jews are like Job in the Bible. We ask God why we are victims of anti-Semitism. Does God intend us to be the Gentiles' scapegoats for their shortcomings and mistakes? Are all creatures predators and we Jews their special prey? Adding to my internal conflict with God and Christians, my daughter married a Christian. They now have a little boy and girl. I wonder whether I can be of help in their religious upbringing without causing any marital trouble between my daughter and her husband. So I am here to learn what you all have to say and whether I can find my future path.

My name is **Thomas**. I come from a non-religious family who thinks religion represents a superstitious crutch for the weak. I belong to no church and have explored the tenets of various faiths, Christianity included. I fortunately have not experienced the trauma Sarah has but feel victimized by Christians for my unbelief. I have fallen in love with a Christian lady whom I would like to marry. But my unbelief and non-religious outsider status with her and her family give both of us pause as to what our future together should or will be. Maybe my time with you can help me. At least I hope so.

My name is **Milton.** I teach philosophy at New York University. I come from an evangelical Christian background. My studies in philosophy challenge many of my current and former religious beliefs. So I spend considerable time studying theologians' and church historians' thoughts and works. I question many of their methodologies and the factual basis for many of their positions. Anita asked me to participate in this group because she thought my training and studies may be of some help to all of you.

You may want to read, study, and discuss these books in a small group setting. At the conclusion of each chapter, there are questions for further consideration. Words in italics can be found in the Glossary.

Chapter 1

Musings/Callings

Now faith is the assurance of things hoped for, the conviction of things not seen. Indeed, by faith our ancestors received approval. By faith we understand that the worlds were prepared by the word of God, so that what is seen was made from things that are not visible.

Hebrews 11:1-3

Anita: Not too long ago I had a dream. I was in the midst of white puffy clouds. Nothing was visible in this mist except for a free hanging sign that read in large letters "CLOSED." Where was I? I turned the sign first one way and then the other. The message never changed.

I wondered: "What's happening? How did I get here? O God, please help me! What should I do? Is this the entrance to your eternal home? Are you barring me from it?"

Then I heard a voice say: "For now."

"What do you mean? Have I not tried to live my life in your service?"

"Yes, but your work is not finished. You must continue writing. Tell people about me and how I made myself known to all who have eyes to see and ears to hear. Speak to them in everyday language. Help them to understand my ways."

"But will they listen to me? Look at the way they treat each other. You have given them their freedom to follow their own desires. You sent Moses and the prophets. You came among us and was crucified by the religious/political establishment of that time. What makes you think I can make a difference? Send someone more convincing than I."

"No! Go to my people. I will be with you. Teach them about me. Help them understand my ways."

"But so many people have already done what you ask me to do. So many people are defiant and will not listen."

"Write!"

"But! But!"

"Write!"

Then I awoke.

This dream has troubled me ever since. Was God really speaking to me and ordering me to write? Had I arrived in some sacred space and was barred from entering? There was no door or door knob only the free hanging sign. In the autumn of my life, is God saying to me that I must complete my work before the sign says "OPEN"? Will I forever be excluded? And from what? Or will I at some future time enter a one-way, no-exit destination somewhere outside planet earth's time and space? And exactly what will it be like? Only time may tell.

Thomas: My skepticism makes it hard for me to believe what you are saying. Do you really think God was communicating with you?

Anita: To you it may only be a meaningless dream. But I wonder why it was so vivid. Are you saying that certain dreams are not allowed? Are they off limits? Can they not be God's way of communicating with us? Can anyone stop dreams from happening?

Thomas: Well, no. But why are you telling us about this dream? Aren't you in effect setting yourself up as some sort of authority or messenger from God?

Anita: Well, you could say that about all clergy and religious people who encounter Jesus in their daily lives. Some see him in other persons, in the frail and vulnerable, and in those workers helping them. All of life is sacred with different meanings and purposes for different people.

Mary: My namesake had an angelic visitation. And Joseph, her husband, had a dream telling him to take baby Jesus and Mary out of harm's way and to go to Egypt.

Thomas: Do you really believe that happened?

Mary: Yes. And with all my heart. There is a spiritual dimension to life which we should be open to. It may not be visible, but it is there. Did you watch Pope Francis during the Mass at Madison Square Garden? Even though he wore elaborate robes, the close-ups of him showed a humble man with a message from the Lord. I challenge anyone to deny his sincerity, mission, and genuineness.

Thomas: It so happens, my girlfriend and I saw this Mass on TV. What amazed me were the looks of joy, wonder, and devotion on people's faces as they gathered in worship. I wish I could feel like them.

Anita: Perhaps in time you may.

Until then, let me share with you some of my musings about my life and God. Early in life, I accepted God's call to be God's voice, heart, hands, teacher, and preacher. This call also led me into ordained ministry as well as to a writing ministry.

I had the good fortune to be married to an extraordinary and adventurous man who opened up for me broader horizons and understandings. My late husband came from six generations of sea captains. His father died when he was eight. He wished to follow their calling. But his family's flight from invading Soviet troops led them to flee their home in Riga, Latvia. After World War II, they spent five years in a Displaced Persons' camp in Germany. No sooner were they resettled in the state of Washington by the Lutheran Church, he was drafted into the Korean War. Upon his return from Korea and Heartbreak Ridge, he used his GI bill to get an education.

His greatest joy in life was family and adventures on the water in his sail boat. Sailors' adventures often are as unpredictable as the weather. They can be life threatening as well as a glorious gift from God. One beautiful summer day, we set sail from Rye, NY, for Shelter Island in Long Island Sound. Near journey's end, the fog rolled in. The wind died. Visibility dropped. Daylight gave way to darkness. My husband turned on the engine and slowly powered ahead. At that time our boat lacked radar and a GPS. But we did have two compasses and a depth finder which my husband used in conjunction with his charts to track our course. I stood on the bow of the boat away from the noise of the engine to listen and look for the entrance bell buoy to Shelter Island. If we couldn't find it, we could land on the rocks or be hit by oncoming boats or rising submarines that ply these waters.

Eventually, I heard the bell buoy. We cautiously approached it. My relief and sense of safety made me want to circle this bell buoy until the fog lifted. But my husband, a fearless yet cautious man, refused. If we stayed there too long, we could run out of diesel as well as be subject to the tide and oncoming boats. He handed me the tiller and went below to plot the compass course into the harbor. By carefully staying on course as well as reading the soundings below, we made our way into the safety of the harbor.

I will never forget this adventure and the lessons I learned from it. They may be helpful to you as well. They are:

- We can't cling to a bobbing bell buoy for safety. It is anchored in one spot. It tosses us about, throws us off balance and leads nowhere. And eventually fatigue and brain fog will overwhelm us. The bell buoy is a navigational marker that locates us in a specific spot. That's all. The direction we take from it is our decision.
- All my husband and I had at our disposal were steady nerves, boating and navigational skills, a safe boat, navigational charts, two compasses, and a depth finder to aid us.
- I view the Bible and its revelations about God as my compass, chart, depth finder, GPS, boat, and habitat for my voyage through life.
- They are like bell buoys and road signs that point us toward our destination. How we use them is our choice. Keep in mind that weather conditions, relationships, limitations, health issues, and other constraints and/or pathways need to be part of the larger framework, too.
- Don't let fear take anchor in your mind. So live, learn and move ahead. Don't just live.

Milton: Your experiences can be instructive and helpful if we want to apply them. But they don't provide all the answers to life.

Anita: You're right. We must use our minds, keep the faith, and dare to go further than we can see or imagine at any given time.

Thomas: Many of us feel lost in life and don't know which direction to take. We are not even sure what our destination should be. There are no simple answers to the challenges we face in today's world. The Bible cannot possibly tell me what decisions I need to make.

Edward: I agree with you Thomas. You need to be careful, very careful. Too many people interpret the Bible from their preferred perspective to justify certain actions, events, and beliefs for which the authors never anticipated or would ever find acceptable. Some people's use of biblical references fails to understand the overall context from which they are taken.

Sarah: That's true. Such behavior has caused the fractures within Judaism and Christianity as well as between Christians and Jews.

Mary: In 1965 and in the wake of World War II, Vatican II promulgated a document called *Nostra Aetate* that recognizes our common ancestry and bond with Jews and their covenant with God. It regrets past hostilities towards Jews and "decries hatred, persecutions, and displays of anti-Semitism, directed against Jews at any time and by anyone." It is unfortunate that more people are not aware of this document.

Anita: *Nostra Aetate* is a very important document that refers to other religions as well. Thank you Mary for drawing our attention to it.

The entirety of Hebrew and Christian scripture is full of peoples' understanding and misunderstanding of their relationship with God. So I ask you to patiently journey with me through the challenges, fog and storms of life as we explore who Jesus is and why he is important to our life's journey.

So come aboard and journey with me.

Think About It

- What are the guiding principles for your life?
- What resources do you use to help you navigate your voyage through life?
- How did you come by them?
- Are they adequate?

Chapter 2

What about Mary?

> *...you will conceive in your womb and bear a son, and you will name him Jesus. He will be great, and will be called the Son of the most high...*
>
> Luke 1:30-31

> *...take Mary as your wife, for the child conceived in her is from the Holy Spirit. She will bear a son, and you are to name him Jesus, for he will save his people from their sins."*
>
> Matthew 1:18-21

Anita: Within Protestantism, Mary's importance is mostly overlooked because of the doctrine of the Virgin Birth promulgated by the Roman Catholic Church. Regardless of what you believe, it is important to consider her rightful place as Jesus' mother. Mary loved Jesus and cared for him as he grew from a baby to a man.

Many of us have different conceptions and beliefs about God and God's role in our lives. The Judeo/Christian conception of God cannot be compared to the philosophers' gods of abstraction and argumentation. We only know God through God's purposeful revelation and interaction with our ancestors and us. God delivered the Israelites from slavery in Egypt. God brought about the Jewish people's second exodus from their forced exile in the land of Babylon. God raised Jesus from the dead. The survival of the Jewish and Christian faith communities continues to this day despite their enemies' efforts to destroy them. No despots can prevent or forestall God's purposes and future from happening. God cannot be controlled by false gods, rulers, and us.

We know Jesus is born into a world ruled by Rome with King Herod and many Temple officials as Rome's collaborators, proxies, and puppets. Collectively they rule the Jewish people. Under these circumstances, the Jews find hope and staying power in the belief that God will send them a *Messiah*, God's anointed. Over time their expectations of the Messiah's power and his role in their deliverance grow. They expect him to throw off all foreign oppressors and to restore Israel to its former glory and power that existed under Kings David and Solomon.

People's expectations fail to take into account God's plans as announced throughout history by God's prophets and then by Jesus. Many think in material and worldly dimensions rather than in spiritual dimensions.

Let us begin by taking a look at John the Baptist's and Jesus' birth narratives. Many scholars believe that these birth narratives found in Matthew and Luke were added to the gospels at a later date.

Thomas: I don't believe these birth narratives to be true. Mary was the only person who could have told her contemporaries about her and Elizabeth's experiences. Mary was perhaps long dead before they were ever composed. Someone wrote these stories to create belief in these unverifiable facts.

Sarah: Thank you Thomas. I agree with you.

Anita: One important feature you need to consider is that these birth narratives as well as the gospels are faith summaries of the early Christian community. Yes, these birth narratives probably were inserted in the gospels at a later date. But the gospel writers wrote from the perspective and knowledge of the importance of Jesus' ministry, crucifixion and resurrection. It is only natural to want to learn more about Jesus' and John's origins. And Mary was alive to tell her story. With the birth of John and Jesus, a paradigm shift occurs. A new order begins to break into the world beginning with the birth of John the Baptist who will call people to a recognition of their sins and a need for confession and repentance. He will be the forerunner for Jesus.

In Luke 1, their stories are tied together beginning with the angelic announcements regarding their special conceptions. First the angel Gabriel appears before the elderly Zachariah who is doing his priestly duty in the Temple. Gabriel tells Zachariah that he and his elderly wife Elizabeth will have a son whom they will call John. He will prepare the people spiritually for the coming of the Messiah. But Zachariah questions how this conception can come to be. He and Elizabeth are too old to have a child. He forgets that his faith ancestors Abraham and Sarah conceive Isaac in their old age. He forgets nothing is impossible for God. Because of his disbelief, Zechariah is made mute until John's naming day.

Milton: By the way, angels are God's messengers. They may take on various forms or no form at all. They supposedly bridge the gap between God and humanity. Only some believers are aware of them. Artists through the ages have drawn them as winged humans, but we do not know what they really look like. In addition to using angels to communicate with people, God sometimes sends word to people through scripture, prophets, dreams and other people.

Anita: Thank you Milton for that information. Six months after visiting Zachariah, Gabriel visits a Jewish peasant maiden named Mary. He tells her that she is favored and blessed among women and has been chosen by God to conceive and bear a son whom she will call Jesus. Gabriel's visit to Mary is known as the *Annunciation.*

Of course Mary wonders how this can occur as she is a virgin. Gabriel tells her, "The Holy Spirit will come upon you, and the power of the Most High will *overshadow* you: therefore the child to be born will be holy; he will be called Son of God."[1] Mary then says, "Here am I, the servant of the Lord; let it be with me according to your word."[2]

Milton: By the way, the term *overshadow* does not refer to divine sexual activity as found in Greek myths of gods impregnating women. By using the Greek term for *overshadow*, Luke emphasizes the miraculous circumstances of Jesus' conception and removes any thoughts of any sexual intercourse. The emphasis here is that Jesus has human and divine origins.

Anita: In other words the entire birth story is not a matter of biology. It is a matter of religious truths and beliefs. Mary represents the faithful of Israel who responds to God's call for humble, loving service.

Thomas: Many people do not believe that Jesus was conceived by the Holy Spirit. It is not verifiable then or now. But did you know that three sisters in England each bought *Immaculate Conception* insurance for 100 pounds a year? This policy would pay out 1,000,000 pounds should they conceive. However in order to recover this insurance money, the burden of proof would be on the sister who conceived in this manner. This pay out would cover the cost of raising a child even though Joseph raised Jesus on a carpenter's income. The Vatican brought an end to this insurance policy affair.

Anita: Let's get serious. Matthew and Luke are very deliberate about Jesus' heavenly origins. Mark and John concentrate on Jesus the man, his mission, crucifixion, and resurrection. The reason Matthew and Luke stress Jesus' divine origin is that they believe Jesus is Emmanuel, God with us, even though Jesus takes on all our human limitations.

Mary: The Catholic Church insists that we believe in the virgin birth. It is important that we recognize Jesus' divinity as well as his humanity.

Anita: That's true. Whatever your belief or acceptance or rejection of these birth narratives, all gospels want to make it clear that Jesus is God who comes to us in the flesh. His incarnation is a new creative act and revelation by God. Matthew and Luke emphasize the virgin birth. They both use genealogies to trace Jesus' origins and pedigree through Joseph who is considered Jesus' legal father. An adopted child has all the rights and status of a biological child. In Luke, Jesus' origins go back to Adam and in Matthew back to King David from whose lineage a Messiah is expected. These gospel writers make the point that Jesus is not a human being whom God adopted at his baptism to be the Son of God as the *Ebionites/Adoptionists*[3] believed. Nor was Jesus a non-material phantom who entered our world who only seemed to be human according to the *Docetists*.[4] Mary is the flesh and blood mother of a flesh and blood son.

Milton: Luke 2 is specific as to the time in history when the events he writes about come to pass. Jesus is born during the reign of Emperor Augustus who ruled from 27 BCE to 14 CE.

Quirinius is Governor of Syria. He orders a census that causes great dislocation to the nation because everyone must return to their ancestral towns. Symbolically, the overcrowded inns represent people and places that have no room for Jesus in their lives and hearts. Jesus' birth in a stable and the shepherds' visit indicate that he comes to the lowly born and those people marginalized by society. They will hear and respond to Jesus' message and call.

Anita: I like Mary and what she represents. She is not a coward. She is a pure and pious Jew who accepts God's call and the challenge to be the mother of the Messiah even without a husband. Someone has to be his mother. She doesn't cling to the illusion of safety in a bobbing bell buoy. By faith alone, she ventures into the fog of an unknown future.

After Gabriel's visit, Mary hastens into the hill country to visit Elizabeth. Upon greeting each other, the unborn John leaps in Elizabeth's womb. Her pregnancy becomes for Mary a divine affirmation of Gabriel's message. Elizabeth knows what Mary's role will be before they even exchange what has transpired. Both women are blessed and filled with the Holy Spirit. In her joy, Mary envisions a reversal of roles for the lowly, the proud, the powerful, the disenfranchised, the hungry, the satiated as only part of her and Jesus' future impact on the world.[5]

Initially, when Joseph learns of Mary's pregnancy, he plans to dismiss her. But the Lord appeared to Joseph in a dream and told him not to be afraid to take her as his wife. The child conceived in her is from the Holy Spirit. She will bear a son, and you are to name him Jesus, for he will save his people from their sins.[6] The spiritually hungry will also be nourished.[7] From this dream, Joseph learns that Jesus will not only save people from their sins but also that Jesus is not after earthly power or dominion.

Mary only learns of the darker side of her and Jesus' future when she takes Jesus to the Temple for his presentation to the Lord and her purification after child birth—all required by the Law of Moses.

Milton: Jews believe the first born son belongs to God. He can be redeemed or bought back by the parents with the payment of five shekels. There is no mention of Mary and Joseph redeeming Jesus. That signifies that Jesus is set apart from others and will dedicate his life to God's work.[8]

Anita: There is an old man named Simeon who was promised by the Holy Spirit that he would not die before he would see the Lord's anointed. When Simeon came into the Temple and saw the baby Jesus, he took him into his arms. Then, inspired by the Holy Spirit he declares:

- Jesus will be the means of salvation for all peoples—Gentiles and Jewish people alike.
- Jesus will bring truth to light and will call people to make a decision whether to follow the light or to live in darkness.
- Decision time will expose people's inner spiritual life.
- Simeon forewarns Mary of the price she and Jesus will have to pay when Jesus begins his ministry.
- Simeon says to Mary that sorrow like a sharp sword will pierce her heart. She will live to bury her son.
- Jesus is born to die a cruel death.[9]

Milton: Also, Anna, a prophetess in the Temple, confirms Simeon's prophetic witness.[10]

Anita: Through their mothers, the gospel writer Luke links John and Jesus together and compares their relationship and different purposes. John will be like the prophet Elijah and will close an era. Jesus will usher in a new one. Both will do the sovereign will of God. Both will seek to save the world by asking people to stop sinning, seek forgiveness for their sins and lead a new, obedient life in God's service. Then the kingdom of God, with its peace and wholeness, will become a reality.

Also, Jesus takes on all our human limitations. That means he can suffer, be hurt, be joyful, and subject to sickness and death. He empties himself of his divinity.

Please note that Mary, Joseph, Zechariah, and Elizabeth are faithful and pious members of the Jewish faith community. God does not choose unbelievers to do God's will. But it is understood that God is with us and calls for our human agency.

Matthew's birth narrative emphasizes the darkness and pain that people experience as the new order breaks into the world.

Milton: That's right. A year or two later Wise Men arrive in Herod's court asking: "Where is the child who has been born king of the Jews? For we observed his star at its rising, and have come to pay him homage."[11] These Wise Men's venture and knowledge frightens Herod. He is Rome's political appointee and wants to continue to hold his position of power. His scribes tell the Wise Men that the prophecies and scripture say that the Messiah will be born in Bethlehem of Judea.

Anita: Indirectly the scribes say that we can't find Jesus without the Hebrew Scriptures to point the way.

Milton: These Wise Men are believed to be astrologers with scientific knowledge. They are men of great wealth and importance. If they were not, they would not have journeyed so far from home laden with valuable gifts to give to Jesus. Nor would they have been admitted into Herod's presence. Contemporary astronomers say that an exploding star or supernova, known as Halley's Comet, did appear in the sky around the time of Jesus' birth.

Anita: Herod intends to yield no ground to a Messiah. When the Wise Men fail to return as requested by Herod to tell him where the Messiah is located, Herod kills approximately 30 baby boys two years old and younger in Bethlehem. Herod figures it probably took a minimum of one year for the Wise Men from Persia or modern-day Iran to reach Bethlehem. We know time has elapsed since Jesus' birth because the Wise Men enter a house and not a stable.[12] After their visit, Joseph is warned in a dream to take Mary and Jesus and flee to Egypt and not to return until told to do so. Herod's Slaughter of the Innocents brings grief, pain, and suffering. It is a foretaste of what will happen to Jesus as a grown man and to his followers. After Herod dies, Joseph is told in a dream to return to Israel. The family returns and settles in Nazareth.

Mary: Jesus and his parents are like modern-day refugees fleeing despots and their deadly massacres.

Anita: That's an excellent observation and comparison.

These births and the advent of a bright star parallel the death of one order and the beginning of another order. Gentiles represented by the Wise Men are included in this new order. They, as well as down-trodden and marginalized Jews, will be able to enter into this new order. That is why Herod tried to stop it from becoming a reality. Power brokers threaten Jesus' life from birth to death. Instead of a throne and crown, Jesus will be executed on a cross with a crown of thorns.

Think About It

- If you were Mary, what would be your reaction to a visitation by the angel Gabriel?
- If you were Joseph, would you heed the angel's warning made to Joseph in a dream?
- Do you think both birth narratives reveal God's mysterious presence and new creative act?
- How is Jesus' entrance to this world similar to our present-day refugee and migrant crisis?

Chapter 3

A Cry in the Wilderness

...The word of God came to John son of Zechariah in the wilderness. He went into all the region around the Jordan, proclaiming a baptism of repentance for the forgiveness of sin...John said to the crowds that came out to be baptized by him, "You brood of vipers! Who warned you to flee from the wrath to come? Bear fruits worthy of repentance. Do not begin to say to yourselves, 'We have Abraham as our ancestor'; for I tell you, God is able from these stones to raise up children to Abraham. Even now the ax is lying at the root of the trees; every tree therefore that does not bear good fruit is cut down and thrown into the fire."

And the crowds asked him, "What then should we do?" In reply he said to them, "Whoever has two coats must share with anyone who has none, and whoever has food must do likewise."

Luke 3: 1-11

Anita: John is now a grown man preaching in the wilderness, away from the large towns and cities. Crowds of people come to hear him. The crowd consists of spectators, the curious, spiritual seekers, and religious establishment informants.

John unsettles all the people by saying that their relationship to Abraham does not exempt them from the need for repentance, for right living and the judgment to come. Their lives and deeds will determine their future. What unites this diverse group is their concern for their salvation in the perilous times in which they live. John tells the people the pathway forward is to seek forgiveness for their sins through repentance and to do God's will. The gateway to God will then be open to them with the coming of the Messiah.

The trip into the wilderness is a reminder of the Israelites' wanderings in the wilderness when God formed them into a faith community that trusted in and obeyed God. The wilderness, in essence, is a place where people can go for spiritual renewal. John's message is:

- Turn away from your sins.
- Repent.
- Be baptized as a sign of your desire to live a new life.
- Share with the needy.
- Then God will forgive you of your sins.

Thomas: Exactly what does John mean by the word "repent?"

Anita: *Repentance* is

- Sorrow for wrongs we have committed.
- An admission of fault.
- An attempt to right the wrongs committed by us.

Then we pray that God and our victims will forgive us of our sins. True repentance brings us into a new and better relationship with God and each other.

John the Baptist is an authentic prophet sent by God. He does not care about being politically correct. He is direct and says what he believes needs to be said. He asks his listeners then and through time all of us, "Who told you that you could escape from the punishment God is about to send?"[13]

Thomas: What type of punishment does John mean?

Anita: Jewish people believed their sacrifices to God of unblemished animals, such as goats and/or bulls, removed their sins. They believed their sins were transferred to the poor animals and with their death or by casting them out into the wilderness, their sins were removed. From this practice, we get the psychological and sociological concept of scapegoating.

In addition, some Jews believed that because they were God's chosen people they would be saved from any punishment for their sins. John tells them not to count on their relationship to Abraham. People are personally responsible for their sins of commission and omission. There will be no cheap grace.

Thomas: So what is cheap grace?

Anita: German theologian Dietrich Bonhoeffer coined this terminology. In 1945, Bonhoeffer was hanged as a Nazi resistor in a Nazi prison camp. He wrote in his book *The Cost of Discipleship* in essence the following:

> Cheap grace means grace sold in the marketplace like shoddy, inferior goods. The sacraments, the forgiveness of sin, and the consolations of religion are thrown away at cut prices. Grace is represented as the Church's inexhaustible treasure, from which she showers blessing with generous hands, without asking questions or fixing limits. Cheap grace is grace without price; grace without cost! The essence of grace, we suppose, is that the account has been paid in advance; and, because it has been paid in full by Jesus, everything can be had for nothing.

> ...Cheap grace is the grace we bestow on ourselves. Cheap grace is the preaching of forgiveness without requiring repentance, baptism without church discipline, Communion without confession, absolution without personal confession. Cheap grace is grace without discipleship, grace without the cross, grace without Jesus Christ.[14]

So what is John the Baptist and Bonhoeffer trying to tell us? People ask John, "What then should we do?" John replies by telling them to share their goods and blessings with others. Tax collectors should not collect more than what is due the government. And soldiers are to be satisfied with their wages and must refrain from extorting money and goods from the people.

Additionally, John insists people should have sorrow for their sins, seek repentance, and turn to God. They and we are to live a new, sin-free life in order to be saved from God's discipline and punishment.

Thomas: Well, what type of punishment does John have in mind?

Anita: John has in mind our eternal lives whether they will be with God or barred from God's presence.

Let me illustrate what John the Baptist may have had in mind. In 1860, Count Leo Tolstoy had a religious conversion experience that caused him to challenge the practices and beliefs of the Russian Orthodox Church. Eventually he was excommunicated for his unorthodox beliefs.

Around the turn of the 20th century, Tolstoy wrote a short story called "The Bus Stop." This story goes as follows.

***

Everyone on the bus heard the blowout of the tire and saw the desperate attempt the bus driver made to keep the bus under his control. He slowed the bus before steering it to the right shoulder of the road. Once the bus came to a full stop, he ordered everyone to leave the bus.

Betty Ann got off the bus with the two children she was caring for. The cold wind whipped through the passengers as they huddled together to talk about their situation. There were a few very poor homes nearby. No one knew who lived in them, nor did they want to know. They decided they could wait out in the cold the hour or so it would take for the tire to be replaced.

Betty Ann was concerned that Joe and Mary, who were seven and eight years old, would get sick in the cold. So she and the children walked over to the nearest shack and knocked on the door. She opened the door without waiting for anyone to open it for her. The inside of the hut was dirty and smoke filled.

Mary and Joe did not notice the dirt. They noticed a boy about Joe's age who was barefoot and had a swollen stomach. A girl about five years old stood in the corner with only a blouse to cover her body. The mother was leaning over a table trying to comfort a crying baby. She left the baby for a few minutes to make Betty Ann and the children comfortable.

Betty Ann took from her bag a thermos of hot chocolate and some rolls. As she poured the hot chocolate into a cup, Mary asked the mother, "Why is your baby crying?"

"Because she is hungry," replied the mother.

"Why don't you give her something to eat?" Mary asked.

"Because we have no food," answered the mother.

Then the babysitter, Betty Ann, called for Mary and Joe to come to the table and drink their hot chocolate and to eat something.

Mary and Joe stood in the middle of the floor almost in a trance. They had never before seen such dirty children with no clothing or no food. They looked at each other and then at the children.

Betty Ann called angrily to them again. “Come now and eat your food and drink your hot chocolate.”

“Give our food and drink to these hungry people,” said Joe.

“Don’t be silly. Come now and do as I tell you. You can give them what is left over.”

Then both children said, “We won’t eat until they are fed.”

Betty Ann poured some hot chocolate out for the baby and other children. Then she turned to Joe and Mary, “Eat what I have set out for you. We can’t help it that God has been generous to your father and mother and not to these people. It is God’s will.”

By now, both Mary and Joe are testy. “It can’t be God’s will. I will not believe it. If God is like that, then I do not want to believe in a God who will let these people be so poor and hungry. It’s horrible how they have to live.”

“If you don’t behave yourselves, I will have to tell your father,” said Betty Ann.

“Go ahead and tell him,” said Mary. “I have made up my mind. It is not fair that some people have so much and other people have little or nothing. God is bad, bad!”

From behind the wood stove, an old man coughed and said, “God is not bad, young lady. It is not God’s fault that some people have a lot and others barely have enough to stay alive. You see, the people with a lot have forgotten what God through John the Baptist and Jesus taught us about sharing what we have with the needy.”

“But what should we do so that everyone has enough of everything?” asked Mary.

"Don't you know?" said the old man. "Do as Jesus taught you: share and share alike."

"That's what I will do when I grow up," said Mary.

"I will too," said Joe.

"Now don't be silly, children. Drink your hot chocolate."

"We won't! We won't! Leave everything here for these people."

"Good for you," said the old man. "You have the right idea. May God bless you."

Just then the bus driver came and announced, "The tire has been changed and we're ready to roll."

Mary and Joe grabbed their thermos and rolls and gave them to the mother. Joe said, "Here keep these. They will help you a little bit."

Betty Ann scolded them both and went to get the things back from the mother, but the children stood in her way. The bus driver was honking on his horn. Betty Ann gave up in disgust and dragged the children to the bus.

***

If John the Baptist's message is correct, what do you think will happen in the future for the likes of Betty Ann, Mary, Joe, and the impoverished family?

Thomas: Wow! That's some story. I do not want to be like the babysitter. She's a cold fish doing her duty towards the children, nothing else. Nor is she setting a good example for them.

Mary: She probably considered herself to be a Christian. But unless she changes her attitude and lack of compassion towards others, she will be excluded from God's kingdom. Doesn't she know we are called to share with the needy?

Milton: Mary and Joe are introduced to poverty and are overwhelmed by it. They are young and impressionable. But this bus stop may sear into their hearts and minds what they can and must do with their lives. They may come to believe that everything belongs to God and that what is in their possession they must share with those who are without. The extremes of poverty and wealth within Russian society may have sown the seeds for the Bolshevik Revolution. Income inequality thrives in most societies and endangers their futures.

Anita: Well said Milton.

Thomas: If I were to put myself in the shoes of that poverty-stricken family and allowed Betty Ann, Mary, and Joe the temporary hospitality in the warmth of my house even though they were uninvited and intruders, I would wonder who in God's world these people are. I would be especially offended by Betty Ann's lack of compassion for my starving family. I gave her hospitality, and she refused to lift a finger to help me and my family's dire needs.

Anita: Then you agree with the old man that God is not responsible for their poverty? It is not God's fault that some people have a lot and others barely have enough to stay alive. The goods of this world were never meant to be had by the few. Like the manna in the wilderness, it cannot be hoarded. We are meant to gather no more than what meets our daily needs. Excess manna becomes corrupted and uneatable.

Thomas: Mary and Joe show us in some small way what we can do to resist evil.

Anita: Yes indeed. I want to say a few more things about John the Baptist before we conclude this meeting. The people who left the city to see and hear John thought that perhaps he was the Messiah. But John tells them he is not the Messiah. He even says that he is unworthy to untie the Messiah's sandals.[15]

John says that the Messiah's baptism will be with the Holy Spirit and with fire. The Holy Spirit and fire are symbols for God's presence and God's judgment. All those who repent of their sins, turn to God, and seek forgiveness need not fear God's judgment, because God will be merciful and forgive them.

Milton: John the Baptist's message to the people is revolutionary. Not since the prophets had anyone spoken so radically. In fact, John is so sure of his mission and message that he verbally attacks King Herod, the son of Herod the Great who was in power when John and Jesus were born. John accuses King Herod of committing adultery, because he married his brother's wife, Herodias. For this offense, Herod arrests John and eventually beheads him.

Anita: Before John is arrested by King Herod, he baptizes Jesus. At our next meeting we will turn to Jesus' baptism by John and Jesus' temptations in the wilderness.

Think About It

- What do you think of John the Baptist's message?
- What is your reaction to Betty Ann, Mary, and Joe and their experience in the shack?
- Is Betty Ann sinning because she did not share?
- How would you feel and act if you were the poor, starving family and well-fed people enter your space and ate before you without sharing what they had with you?
- Does this happen today? Where?
- Is God to blame for starvation? What makes you think so?

Chapter 4

Here Comes Jesus

> *The greatest temptations are not those that solicit our consent to obvious sin, but those that offer us great evils masking as the greatest good.*
>
> *No Man Is an Island*
> Thomas Merton

Anita: The hidden years of Jesus' private preparation for proclaiming the good news from God give us little information about his life before his baptism by John the Baptist. Two scenes in the Temple tell us that Jesus was raised as a practicing Jew—when he was presented to God as a new born and when at age 12 he stayed behind after the Passover Festival to converse with teachers in the Temple.

John the Baptist is like Elijah who tries to prepare people for the Day of the Lord. In the wilderness, he calls out to those who wish to enter God's kingdom that they must first demonstrate repentance for their sins and have a new heart. John says that no moral law, no privately held belief, and no ritual will cleanse people of their sins without genuine repentance for them. Once they have repented and turned from their sinful ways, they can cleanse themselves with his baptism.

His preaching and baptism mark a dramatic paradigm shift from a system of strict legal observances of Jewish laws to an attitude of uncompromising sincerity. John calls people to remove, to discard all that block their knowing the Lord. Only by knowing the Lord and doing the Lord's work can anyone enter eternal bliss.

Thomas: So why does Jesus seek baptism from John the Baptist? Isn't Jesus supposed to be sinless and have no need of baptism?

Anita: That's true. But I believe John's baptism of Jesus tells us many things about him:

- It anoints Jesus for ministry and becomes a model for Christian baptism.
- Jesus aligns himself with God's purpose. He aligns himself with needy, repentant sinners and their spiritual needs.
- Jesus is anointed by the Holy Spirit as were we at our baptism. Christian baptism is the rite in which we believe God pledges the permanent presence of the Holy Spirit in our lives. God does not force God's will on us. We can cooperate or not cooperate with God.
- Jesus intends to live within our human limitations and therefore limits the use of his divine power.
- Also since Jesus is limited by his humanity, he is now assured of his union with God when a voice from heaven says: "This is my Son, the Beloved, with whom I am well pleased."
- Jesus' and our baptism start us on our path as God's servants in this world. Jesus and the baptized in his name are commissioned for discipleship and something greater than themselves.

Jesus' behavior tells us we need to think carefully about how we program our GPS and destination for our future course in life. After Jesus' baptism, he is led by the Holy Spirit into the wilderness.

Thomas: Wait a minute. Who or what is this *Holy Spirit*?

Anita: The Holy Spirit is God's invisible presence with us.

Mary: The wilderness is a good place to think away from the noise and distractions of the world. It is a place for spiritual renewal. The silence and peace found there give us time to think and commune with God.

Milton: Yes, but the wilderness can be a frightening place as well. In the wilderness, there is a struggle for survival. Life and death issues stand out in all their starkness. The trappings of society do not hide them. So life takes on new meaning in this harsh environment. We ask ourselves whether we are to live only for the sake of survival, as the animals do. What would life be like then? Or whether we are to live in such a way that we fulfill God's purposes for us? What would life be like then?

Anita: Often when we have big decisions to make, we need time to be alone, to think, and to pray about the decisions we will ultimately make. It is believed that Jesus purposefully went into the wilderness to think and pray about what shape his ministry would take.

The gospels tell us Jesus fasted for 40 days in the wilderness. This fasting meant that he probably took water and little else.

Milton: He could not have survived without water, because he would become dehydrated and die. Jesus was just as human as we are. By the way, whenever the number 40 is used in the Bible, it means a long time and not literally 40 days.

Anita: Yes. After a long time in the wilderness, Jesus is famished and the devil tempts him. When we speak of the tempter or the devil or Satan, we really are talking about evil that is personified. Satan is the name we give to a person or will that is actively hostile to God.

Milton: The concept of evil personified was borrowed from Zoroastrian beliefs. This personification carried forward into the New Testament and into Christian doctrines of the Atonement. Many Protestants have abandoned this concept of a personified evil power as a relic of pre-scientific thinking, although many find the symbolism still to be useful. Medieval art expressed people's concept of evil incarnate as an ugly, red-horned semi-human creature carrying a pitchfork.

Anita: Yes, but modern art and literature are different. Evil is now often personified in attractive, tempting forms such as gorgeous, seductive female and male bodies and the thrills they create. Many people today believe that evil appears attractive, because people are not drawn to something ugly or repulsive. They must give in to the seductive power of evil before it can have power over them. Evil can also be found in the distorted ideologies and illusions of a Hitler, Stalin, ISIS, Boko Haram, Kim Jong Un, and terrorists of all kinds.

The gospel writer Matthew uses the literary device of an imaginary debate by Jesus with the forces of evil represented by the devil. This debate also outlines temptations and internal struggles we have and decisions we must make in life.

For a temptation to be real, there must be the possibility of choice. God has given us free choice with the ability to do right or wrong. By rejecting each temptation made by the devil, Jesus makes a conscious choice as to the shape his ministry will take.

The first temptation deals with our bodies. Jesus is hungry, really hungry. The tempter comes and says: "If you are the Son of God, command these stones to become loaves of bread."[16] This temptation challenges Jesus' very identity with the word "IF." Jesus doesn't take the bait. Instead he answers with a quotation from Deuteronomy 8:3 by saying:

> Man does not live by bread alone, but that man lives by everything that proceeds out of the mouth of the Lord.

In other words, the Word of God feeds the spiritually hungry and is more important than material things. If bread alone satisfies people, then they are no better than animals. Hunger and poverty in Israel were no different from what they are in today's world. A bread and butter relationship leads to a master-slave relationship. Obedience to God then would not be out of love but rather out of a fear of losing one's meal ticket. Jesus rejects this means for converting the world to God's ways.

Mary: I think that is why Jesus never bribed his followers with material things but encouraged self-sacrifice.

Milton: That's true. Material things, including food, will not bring people closer to God. This temptation reminds me of political leaders who make promises they can't deliver. Or if they are met, these promises are on the backs of other people.

Thomas: Such as?

Milton: An extreme example is ISIS' recruiting tactics. Their fighters are rewarded with captured and enslaved women who become imprisoned sex slaves.

Anita: That's a good illustration for luring male recruits by bribing them with females to satisfy their sexual fantasies and needs.

These are horrific crimes committed on the backs of innocent people. Just imagine your daughter, sister, or mother as one of these imprisoned sex slaves.

Thomas: Someone close to me was caught in a similar web.

Anita: Tell us about it.

Thomas: Not now. I don't want to talk about it. I wonder why God allows such evil to thrive at the expense of innocent people. That's why I am here. I am trying to understand who Jesus is and if he is the answer to my questions and concerns.

Anita: O.K. We will respect your privacy. But let me say what little I have come to understand about evil. We can't explain it or its origin. It is a perversion of good and a parasite that preys upon the good. Evil is like a fast-growing cancer that must be defeated before it multiplies and kills us. We will revisit this issue of evil time and time again in Jesus' ministry.

Now let us turn to Jesus' next temptation that deals with our souls and pride. Somehow Jesus imagined the devil took him out of the wilderness to the pinnacle of the Temple. It is inconceivable to me that Jesus flew around in the air with the devil. But we must remember these temptations are nothing more than a literary device used by Matthew to convey important truths to us about Jesus.

Again, the tempter is taunting Jesus to identify himself with that word "IF." "If you are the Son of God, create a great spectacle by jumping off the pinnacle of the Temple. God's angels will catch you before you hit bottom. Jesus, this spectacle will win everyone over to you. I have the inside track. Trust me! Come on now! Do it!"[17]

Jesus' response is that you shall not tempt the Lord your God. Spectacles and miracles may mislead people, but they do not create an enduring true faith. Jesus wants people to respond to his message and to whom he is. We are not to use God for our benefit. We are called to a life of service. Jesus will not jump through the devil's or our hoops and false expectations.

Milton: Also, some people would then suspect that Jesus is in league with the devil.

Mary: That's what some of the scribes accused Jesus of.[18] I believe Jesus came to save people from their sins. He came to show us God's love through his actions, miracles, parables, and preaching.

Anita: I agree completely with you. Jesus' miracles were never performed as a recruitment tactic. He sought to heal and feed the spiritually sick and hungry. Jesus wanted to give people hope in hopeless situations.

For argument sake, let us suppose Jesus were incarnate today and accepts the devil's challenge, declares himself the Messiah, and announces he would prove his identity by jumping off the new World Trade Center in lower Manhattan. Can you image the excitement this generates in people, in the mass media, and in social media? Helicopters circle overhead. Crowds anxiously await Jesus' jump. Cameramen push and shove everybody out of their way to get the best location to video tape Jesus' jump. Reporters interview people on the street. Other reporters ask Jesus why he chose this method to reveal that he is the Messiah. Firemen have safety nets in readiness. And the Mayor orders the police not to let Jesus jump without a proper permit.

Jesus jumps. His fall is suspended in mid-air above the firemen's safety nets. He walks in the air pass them and lowers himself into the crowd. What then? Some people will come to Jesus out of fear and not out of love. Others want to be part of his inner circle so they can achieve status and power through him over others. Hollywood agents try to get Jesus to sign a four-year contract. And still others just shrug their shoulders and say it was just another spectacular media stunt signifying nothing.

No enduring belief and faith would come from this spectacle. These same people will not pick up their cross and follow Jesus to his cross. All will abandon him as did Peter who denied even knowing Jesus. He had no intentions to disguise God's purposes through spectacles. Jesus was taking the direct approach. He wanted people to accept and follow him by responding to his message and call to service. Purity of heart and intention are what counts.

Perhaps the third temptation of greed and power is the greatest. The devil is now claiming to be in charge of the entire universe. He offers Jesus the world on the condition that Jesus worships him. This temptation has overtones of military rule and/or dictatorship and forced allegiance. It is a temptation to manipulate and secure power over other people. Why do you suppose Jesus rejects this approach to his ministry?

Milton: North Korea represents how evil works through might and power over its citizens and the sabre rattling towards South Korea and the world. Jesus wants to bring the minds, hearts, and souls of people into union with God. He wants people to worship only God and not the "dear leader" who sets himself up as a god and insists that his brain-washed citizens do as he orders or face death, torture or the work camps.

Anita: I agree. Jesus does not want to establish a kingdom full of violence and oppression. Jesus refuses to seek desirable ends by unworthy means. Idolatrous worship of power and material things will not be part of Jesus' ministry and God's kingdom. Greed and power create an impenetrable wall between God and people. Jesus wants to save people by conquering the evil that exists in their hearts and minds. He wants everyone to repent, seek and serve the Lord our God and serve only God.

Jesus will not allow evil into his spiritual world by succumbing to the temptations of the devil. The evil that existed in Jesus' world overpowered him and brought him to the cross. As in the past and today such evil costs Christians and other minorities their lives.

Mary: The story of Jesus' temptations is our story, too. We are all vulnerable and vacillate when it comes to our bodily and spiritual needs, our sense of self-importance, and our need for status and power over others.

Anita: You are right. Jesus lived a life of self-sacrifice and self-denial. He no doubt shared his temptations with his disciples to warn them of similar temptations they may have. Recall the disciples' quarrel over who was to be regarded as the greatest.[19] Disciples who broker about power rather than lead sacrificial lives of service will lose their effectiveness and perhaps be cast out of Jesus' service. We need to keep in mind that people must give in to the seductive power of evil before it can have power over them. Beyond our survival needs, it is important to remember Jesus' admonition to his disciples when he says:

> If any man would come after me, let him deny himself and take up his cross and follow me. For whoever would save his life will lose it, and whoever loses his life for my sake will find it. For what will it profit a man, if he gains the whole world and forfeits his life?[20]

If we decide to follow Jesus and travel his pathway, we need to remember that the world crucified him once and does so daily. It is difficult to live as a Christian and to resist these three temptations in our life's journey.

Jesus aligns himself with sinners and their spiritual hunger. He aligns himself with God's will and purposes. This alignment covers three important dynamics for discipleship. They are repentance, moral cleansing, and testing. Jesus' message is not about self. It is about self-giving.

If we accept Jesus' invitation, he will help us navigate the uncertain days and years ahead. He says:

> Come to me, all who labor and are heavy laden, and I will give you rest. Take my yoke upon you, and learn from me; for I am gentle and lowly in heart, and you will find rest for your soul. For my yoke is easy, and my burden is light. Amen.[21]

Think About It

- What do you think of the saying "Man does not live by bread alone?"
- Do you believe in the devil and/or evil personified? If so, give us some examples.
- Of what importance are spectacles in winning the minds and hearts of people?
- How are Jesus' temptations similar to our daily temptations?
- Do you agree with Jesus' resistance toward these temptations? Why or why not?
- Why is the third temptation of greed and power the greatest of the three?
- Do you agree with Thomas Merton when he says, "The greatest temptations are not those that solicit our consent to obvious sin, but those that offer us great evils masking as the greatest good." Why do you think so?

Chapter 5

Jesus' Ministry Begins

He comes to us as One unknown, with a name, as of old, by the lake-side, He came to those men who knew Him not. He speaks to us the same word: "Follow thou me!" and sets us to the tasks which he has to fulfil for our time. He commands. And to those who obey Him, whether they be wise or simple, He will reveal Himself in the toils, the conflicts, the sufferings which they shall pass in His fellowship, and, as an ineffable mystery, they shall learn in their own experience Who He is.

Albert Schweitzer

Anita: Jesus leaves the wilderness filled with the Holy Spirit and with the shape of his ministry firmly set in his mind. He begins in the well-populated fertile region known as Galilee which is crisscrossed with heavily traveled trade routes. Here people are known for their courage, subversive opposition to rulers, and openness to new and foreign ideas. Jesus is first known as a rabbi or teacher because he started his ministry teaching in their synagogues—a place where people studied scripture, met for prayer, and where boys were educated. Common people like to hear Jesus because he teaches as a person with authority and not as the scribes who justify their teachings by reciting spiritual authorities.

Jesus calls disciples who have different backgrounds, skills, personalities, and talents. His first disciples Peter, Andrew, James, and John are fishermen. They leave everything behind and join him. His disciples are employed, common folk looking for the Messiah and a new day for Israel. They definitely do not live in palaces and mansions. Jesus, like all teachers of his time, gathers students around him with the understanding that they in turn would someday teach others.

When he is teaching in the Capernaum synagogue, a man cursed with an unclean spirit cries out: "What have you to do with us, Jesus of Nazareth? Have you come to destroy us? I know who you are, the Holy One of God."[22]

Thomas: Who is "us?" Why would Jesus destroy "them?"

Milton: They are the unclean spirits that recognize who Jesus is and feared Jesus' power would cast them out of their prey. Did you know that in Jesus' time, there was a widespread belief in demons, witches, and the like? Even in colonial America, people believed in witchcraft. There were witch trials and executions in Salem, Massachusetts.

Sarah: In the past, people believed that evil forces were numerous and ruled by the devil that they also called Satan, Baalzebub, and Beelzebub. These last two names are derived from the name of a Philistine god. The Israelites considered this god an unworthy rival of God. Other names for Beelzebub were "lord of the flies" and "lord of dung." People believed these evil and hostile forces were capable of living inside people. They thought the evil forces created disorders such as blindness, deafness, and mental illnesses.

Edward: That's true. Superstitions abounded during Jesus' time.

Thomas: And still do today.

Edward: Archaeologists have found numerous skulls with a hole drilled in them. The piece of removed skull was tied to a necklace that people wore around their neck to ward off evil spirits. This behavior was in response to the common belief that the only way people could get rid of demons that possessed them was to provide a passageway out of the body.

Sarah: It's a wonder such procedures didn't kill them with infections.

Anita: People who witnessed Jesus' first miracles and exorcisms tell others how Jesus defeated evil. Soon everyone comes to Jesus for a cure of their ailments. His healing of a man with leprosy causes the man to spread the word about his cure by Jesus. This, in turn, makes it impossible for Jesus to go into towns because of the crush of people seeking cures. Mostly, people were seeking their well-being. Little or no faith in Jesus and his message developed based on his miracles.

Thomas: Isn't our well-being what we are all about. What's wrong with that? Also, I am not so sure I believe in miracles. We could say that modern-day medicine is a miracle.

Anita: In a way today's doctors and medical researchers use their God-given talents to make people well. Just the other day I had an infection and antibiotics quickly made me well. You could say these medicines are miracle drugs. But during Jesus' time, doctors lacked the knowledge, means, and tests to pin point a medical problem and the medicine to cure it. Often people died from infections, diseases, and ignorant medical practices.

Thomas: How would you describe a *miracle*?

Anita: Miracles are wonders and signs from God. They occur outside the laws of nature as we know them. They reveal significant, spontaneous, previously unknown laws of nature. People who are able to perform miracles are specially gifted with God's spirit and power. Moses and various prophets performed miracles. With Moses, we have the ten plagues in Egypt, the dividing of the Red Sea, and the daily supply of manna in the wilderness.

Milton: And Daniel survived the lion's den.

Anita: Yes. Miracles reveal God's presence and divine intervention in history which are outside our ordinary experience and control. Miracles cannot be examined under a microscope. Rarely are they repeatable. We should not ask how Jesus' miracles happened, but rather what message or clue God is giving us, and what the miracles mean for our faith.

When Jesus returns home to Nazareth, people are curious about what he will say and do among them. Will he heal their sick as he has done elsewhere? As was his custom on the Sabbath day, he goes to Nazareth's synagogue where the official known as the Chazzan gives Jesus Isaiah's scroll. Jesus opens the scroll to Isaiah 61:1-2 and reads:

> The Spirit of the Lord is upon me, because he has anointed me to bring good news to the poor. He has sent me to proclaim release to the captives and recovery of sight to the blind, to let the oppressed go free, to proclaim the year of the Lord's favor.[23]

Jesus then sits down and returns the scroll to the Chazzan. He startles everyone by saying, "Today this scripture has been fulfilled in your hearing."[24] That means Jesus claims for himself to be the fulfillment of Isaiah's prophesy and that God's Spirit is upon him. The purpose of his ministry is to bring good news to the poor in spirit, the spiritually blind, and a message of hope and freedom to captives and the oppressed.

In essence, Jesus outlines his mission. He wants to redeem the world and conquer the evil that exists in people's hearts and minds. Love of the material world and pride separates people from God and enslaves them. Love of God frees people and brings people into communion with God.

At first, listeners think well of him. They think their long-awaited liberation and the year of the Lord's favor will begin. Then they question how Jesus, a carpenter's son, could have this wisdom and could affect such a change. They wonder how the Spirit of the Lord could be upon him and anoint him for mission.

Reading their thoughts, Jesus goes on the offensive by saying among other things that:

- No prophet is accepted in his home town.
- Even the prophets Elijah and Elisha came to the aid of non-Jews thereby suggesting that Gentiles will also be included in the year of the Lord's favor.
- Charity begins wherever the need may be and not with any given class or race or religious group.

Thomas: So what was their reaction towards Jesus and his sense of mission?

Anita: An outburst of nationalistic fervor and possibly a sense of superiority seize and enrage the Nazarenes. They expel Jesus from their synagogue and Nazareth. They even attempt to throw him off a cliff. Somehow Jesus "passed through the midst of them and went on his way."[25] It is believed he never returned to Nazareth.

This event introduces the conflict and controversy Jesus will have with Jewish religious authorities and some fellow Jews. Too many of them are wed to the old order and way of thinking and reject him and his teachings.

The pattern of Jesus' ministry as it is stated in the Gospel of Luke goes as follows.

- Jesus is God's servant, God's anointed, who announces to Israel that God reigns over all creation, and God's reign is to be exercised through pardon, healing, liberation, and amnesty.
- Jesus announces that a new age begins with him.
- He has harsh criticism for those in power.
- His message is for the poor and the captives such as the bonded slaves and the oppressed.
- His message is also a warning of judgment to those who oppress or fail to help them.

In Mark 1:14-15 we are given a compressed message as to Jesus' purpose when he says, "The time is fulfilled, and the kingdom of God has come near, repent, and believe in the good news." There is a sense of urgency in this call.

Thomas: What is this good news? And where is the Kingdom of God?

Anita: The *good news* is the message Jesus proclaims as well as the content of his ministry. *Gospel* is also another name for good news.

Thomas: O.K. What then is the meaning of the Kingdom of God?

Anita: In the Synoptic Gospels of Matthew, Luke, and Mark, the expressions the *Kingdom of God* or the *Kingdom of Heaven* refer to the following beliefs commonly held by the Jewish people of Jesus' time.

- The Kingdom of God is a spiritual kingdom where God's universal rule reigns. Everyone will acknowledge God's reign, and a new era of righteousness and peace will begin.
- The Kingdom brings with it a transformation of society as well as of the individual. There is a reordering of peoples' lives in their relation to one another and to God.

Jesus teaches that the way to bring this kingdom into existence is not by rebellion but by a greater righteousness. It is not political in nature. Jesus does not advocate the overthrow of the Romans. He does not find the yoke of the Romans as bad as he finds the yoke of the priests, scribes, and Pharisees. When the Kingdom of God comes into existence, both the yokes of the Romans and of the religious order will be broken.

Matthew's gospel adds another dimension to the understanding of the Kingdom of God. Matthew's community believed that Christianity was the new Law and that the Christian community was the New Israel.

Sarah: We Jews vehemently disagree. Christians are not the New Israel. And God's kingdom has not become a reality.

Anita: I am just telling you the positions of the different gospel writers. In Mark, the Rule of God is in the process of being asserted. God is setting people free and reconciling them to Godself. Luke believes that the Kingdom of God grows unseen within us and is a spiritual kingdom. It has a present and a future quality to it. When all human hardness of heart or disbelief dissolves, God's reign will begin and will overthrow all evil things.

Sarah: But it has not happened yet.

Anita: For some it has.

In the Gospel of John, the *Kingdom of God* is equated with the gift of eternal life, with the coming of the Comforter, or the Holy Spirit. The Kingdom of God is a present and spiritual reality with a future dimension to it.

In Revelation 21:10, the Kingdom of God is "the holy city of Jerusalem coming down out of heaven from God." There is a reordering of peoples' lives in their relation to one another and to God.

Remember the gospels are written faith summaries of the early church. They were written after Jesus' death and resurrection and from a post-crucifixion and Easter vantage point. The first three gospels known as the synoptic gospels are similar to each other. The Gospel of Mark is the oldest and shortest gospel in the New Testament. Luke and Matthew's gospel use much of Mark's material and expand it when they wish to emphasize or reinterpret something that Mark had written.

The Gospel of John was written much later (c. 90-120 CE) than the synoptic gospels and was revised numerous times by other writers before it was put into its final form. John's gospel is the most difficult to understand because of its extensive use of metaphors, symbols, and signs. There are many levels of meaning to everything that is presented in this gospel. Books have been written attempting to explain the opening chapter of John. Its symbolism represents various interpretations compacted into very few words. For instance, what do the opening words in John 1 mean to you?

Mary: For me, the opening words are similar to the opening words of Genesis 1. God is in the beginning creating and giving light. Jesus was with God then. Also, God is breaking out of the holy places to dwell with us in the person of Jesus.

Milton: The use of *Word* tells us that Jesus is part of the power of God that creates and gives life and light. Jesus existed before time, before creation of the universe. *Word* can also be traced to Lady Wisdom[26] and to Greek philosophy. By calling Jesus the Word, John is informing us that Jesus knows where he is from and where he will return. The Word is divine and came to expression in history in the person of Jesus Christ. The humanization of the Word is in John 1:14. "And the Word became flesh and lived among us." The Word is Jesus' thought or self-expression. Jesus partakes of the nature of God and thereby preserves Jewish monotheistic beliefs.

Anita: When John says Jesus is the *Light* of the World, he refers to the divine illumination of a person's mind and conscience. This light dispels human darkness and continues throughout time. The word *Life* refers to the function of the Holy Spirit that represents the positive aspects of life and existence. Life represents the authentic existence God wants us to have. Life and salvation are associated with light.

Darkness is symbolic of unbelief as well as total evil that cannot overcome the Word. Jesus comes into the world as a human being to have a flesh and blood relationship with us. Jesus partially reveals to us the mind of God. As the Word, Jesus brings light into our midst to dispel the darkness; but many turn their backs on the light.

We are called to continue Jesus' work of healing the spiritually, mentally, physically and emotionally sick. We are to free slaves, the falsely imprisoned and tortured, the terrorized, the intimidated, and victims of human trafficking, debt slavery, poverty, ignorance, unemployment or underemployment. We are to welcome and help widows, orphans, and refugees. In other words discipleship calls us to help the needy, the spiritually and physically hungry, the disenfranchised, the starving, the hopeless, and victims of brutality and predatory practices in this world. We believe this is God's call to us as revealed to us through Jesus.

That's a big commitment. Jesus asks us to turn away from our old habits and beliefs to a total commitment to him and his ways. Will we?

Think About It

- How do you think Jesus established his ministry and following?
- Why would anyone accept Jesus or consider him special?
- Why would his disciples give up their livelihood to be itinerant followers of Jesus?
- How did Jesus fulfill his call to ministry as given in the gospel of Luke in the Nazareth synagogue?

Chapter 6

Jesus' Miracles and Their Message

If you think you are beaten, you are;
If you think you dare not, you don't;
If you'd like to win, but think you can't,
It's almost a cinch you won't.

If you think you'll lose, you're lost,
For out in the world we find
Success begins with a person's faith;
It's all in the state of mind.

Life's battles don't always go
To the stronger or faster hand;
They go to the person
Who trusts in God
And always thinks "I can."

Napoleon Hill

Anita: We gain great insight into Jesus' message and mission from what he says and what he does. Therefore, let us examine a few of Jesus' miracles and what they tell us about him. They are categorized as exorcisms, cures, control over nature, and raising the dead.

As we already learned, Jesus' first healing miracle is the healing of a man afflicted with "demon possession." Jesus is God's authority incarnate. Even so, this exorcism produces no converts and no faith in Jesus. His defeat of evil forces at the very beginning of Jesus' ministry implies that Jesus has come to destroy evil by word command and not through violence. His exorcism of the demon heals the man's spirit and enables him to live life fully with others and with God.

The difference between this miracle and the healing of the paralytic[27] that follows is that you cannot be well physically without spiritual, psychological, and emotional health and wholeness. Jewish homes during Jesus' time had a flight of stairs on the outside of their buildings. Roofs were flat and made of sticks and mud. Because the paralytic is paralyzed and the crowds that fill the house Jesus is in blocks his friends from carrying him into Jesus' presence through the ground floor door, they dig through the roof and lower him on his mat into Jesus' presence. "When Jesus sees their faith, he says to the paralytic, "Son, your sins are forgiven."[28] The Jewish leaders present consider his statement blasphemous. They believe only God can forgive sins.

Milton: You see, the priests had an elaborate sacrificial system all worked out from which they made their livelihood. By forgiving the paralytic of his sins, Jesus upsets the machinery or management of forgiveness of sins.

Anita: Yes. Jesus not only heals the paralytic spiritually but authenticates his authority on earth to forgive sin by physically healing him.

In John 5:1-18, Jesus encounters a lonely, sick man beside the Pool of Bethsaida who has waited for 38 years to be cured if only he can be the first person in the water when it is stirred. Jesus asks the man, "Do you want to be made well?" The man does not give Jesus a direct answer such as, "Of course I want to be made well." Instead he gives Jesus an excuse. Jesus orders him to "Stand up, take your mat and walk." But it is the Sabbath. If he does what Jesus tells him to do, he will be violating the Sabbath, a day of rest. He will be violating the legalism of his day. Besides, this man may have tried numerous times to get up and without success.

The man does as Jesus instructs him and is made well. This paralyzed man reminds me of the miracles that occur among the disabled and the handicapped. Many are veteran amputees. Some suffer from traumatic brain injury, post-traumatic stress disorder or neurological disorders, spinal bifida, etc. They do not let their disability define them. They compete in adaptive sports and recreation such as wheelchair hockey, billiards, softball, jousting tournaments, basketball, rugby, water sports, bowling, as well as hand cycling.

Thomas: I have heard about these groups. They help each other and are not isolated in some room feeling sorry for themselves. They have comradery with each other as well as mentor handicapped children to develop their potential and independence. They build their own bridges to a productive future.

Sarah: This man on the mat could be any of us. Maybe he wants to get well but maybe not. He may like the paralysis of self-pity and the comfort he gets from other people. He may not know how to assume adult responsibility and accountability. Life may be less complicated if he remains on his stretcher.

Anita: Yes. Some disabilities, not all, are about attitude and a state of mind. There is a hidden activity of God going on inside these special people as well as from the outside. As Thomas just mentioned, these handicapped people feel good about themselves and what they have accomplished. Their patience and persistence have rewarded them with a new life. And it often comes through another person. That willingness to defy the odds and to help oneself and each other is the real miracle.

Mary: You do what you have to do when you have to do it even if it is on the Sabbath. Jesus says, "The Sabbath was made for humankind, and not humankind for the Sabbath; so the Son of Man is lord even of the Sabbath."[29]

Anita: Good. Another healing miracle is when Jesus restores sight to a man born blind from birth found in John 9. Before we examine this miracle it is important to understand Jewish hostility towards followers of Jesus.

By the time the Gospel of John is written at the end of the first century and the beginning of the second century, hostilities between Jewish leaders and Christians were at an all-time high. This hostility is reflected in John's gospel. Followers of Jesus are expelled from Jewish places of worship. Expulsion from the Jewish faith community meant social as well as religious ostracism and isolation. Jewish converts to Christianity did not make their decisions lightly because their religious community represented a large part of their lives. Christians eventually organized and formed their own faith communities.

It was a common belief that the blind man's blindness is attributed to either the man's sin or his parent's sin. Jesus, as did Job and Ezekiel, refuses to accept sickness and blindness as spiritual defects.

This miracle, performed on the Sabbath, points to Jesus and to the cost of discipleship. Jesus uses his own spit and made mud with it. He puts this mud on the man's eyes and tells him to go to the pool of Siloam to wash it off. Why did Jesus perform this miracle in this fashion?

Sarah: It is the Sabbath. Jesus' making mud or spittle is classified as work and considered a sin and a violation of the Law. It seems Jesus opposes that Law.

Milton: By the way, people believed spittle had healing powers.

Edward: Jesus resists the extremes of the Law regarding the Sabbath. He tests the man's willingness to try anything to gain his sight.

Anita: Good. We have different levels of blindness and sight in this story. Who are the blind and who are the sighted ones?

Mary: The blind man is physically blind. Once his sight is restored and in a short amount of time, he progressively gains spiritual sight. At first, the healed blind man does not know who Jesus is. But by the end of this event, he recognizes Jesus as one from God. You could say that this progression from physical and spiritual blindness to sight is a part of our journey to God and new life.

Milton: I agree. Also, the neighbors are spiritually blind. Rather than rejoice that this blind man can now see, they join with the Pharisees. It could be because this former blind man is no longer humble and dependent on their hand-outs.

Anita: Another problem emerges. Yes, the blind man is blessed, but his new sight exacts from him continued social isolation because he now believes in Jesus. The blind man's parents straddle the fence. They show no joy at their son's new found sight since they fear expulsion from the synagogue. Self-interest and not their son's best interest govern their behavior.

Why does Jesus call the authorities blind?

Mary: They have physical sight to see, but are spiritually blind.

Edward: They are only concerned with the fact that Jesus performed an unauthorized miracle in violation of the Law. They think he is an upstart.

Milton: The Pharisees and authorities lack compassion. They cannot think or see beyond the legalistic framework that imprisons them spiritually. The authorities are so filled with suspicion and a false sense of power that they shut out the Light of the World and continue to live in inner darkness.

Anita: The Gospel of John links this recovery of sight symbolically to light and darkness, day and night, salvation and damnation.

All four gospels feature Jesus feeding 4,000-5,000 men. Women and children are not included in that estimate of the male count. As Jesus' ministry grows, he avoids populated areas and seeks rest in the quiet of deserted places. He travels by boat on the Sea of Galilee from one place to another. Once people spot him, they spread the word as to his whereabouts; and they come to him from all the towns. Jesus has compassion for them because they are like sheep without a shepherd. So he teaches them many things and offers them a purpose for their lives.

One evening, his disciples ask Jesus to send the people away to the towns to get some food. Instead Jesus tells his disciples to feed them and to find out how many loaves the people have. They find five loaves and two fish. The crowds have been with him three days and have eaten their food supplies which they carried with them.[30] Jesus has them sit on the green grass which indicates it must be spring time. They sit in groups of hundreds and fifties.

Then Jesus takes the five loaves and two fish. He looks up to heaven, blesses and breaks the bread and divides the fish and gives them to his disciples to distribute to the people. All are fed. And they collected 12 baskets of left overs.

Remember, miracles are clues to God's activities. What can we learn from this feeding of the 5,000?

Mary: This miracle shows Jesus' concern and compassion for the people and prefigures Jesus' Last Supper and the Eucharist. Table fellowship then becomes a symbol for solidarity.

Milton: Jesus is more than a shepherd king like David and more than Moses through whom God fed the people in the wilderness. Through Jesus, God's power is revealed.

Anita: Symbolically, Jesus nourishes the people with the food of immortality which is eternally satisfying yet the people react on a superficial level. They want to crown him king, a king who will oppose Rome. Therefore, Jesus withdraws from them.

The next day the crowds seek him out. The people want more bread from him. Jesus tells them to seek eternal food and not food that temporarily fills the belly.

Thomas: Does eternal food refer back to Jesus' temptations in the wilderness?

Anita: Yes it does. Jesus tells them that he is the bread of life. The people fail to understand that Jesus is that eternal food. Many are unwilling to look for a deeper meaning in what Jesus has to say and does. To receive Jesus as the bread of life is to receive him and his teachings.

Thomas: Could not the people have shared their food that they carried with them from their homes?

Anita: That is a possibility. But I doubt it. After three days in the wilderness, little food would be left over. So far we have examined a couple of Jesus' healings and the feeding of the 5,000. Before leaving this discussion on miracles, I would like for us to look at Jesus' raising of Lazarus from the dead and what that tells us about Jesus and the fall-out from it.

In John 11, Lazarus of Bethany, a friend of Jesus, falls ill. His sisters Mary and Martha send for him. Rather than rush to Lazarus' side, Jesus stays a few days longer before making the trip to Bethany. Temple hostility towards Jesus has by this time reached a dangerous point. His disciples are concerned that Jesus and they might be stoned to death by Temple proxies if they were to return to Bethany. Jesus knows that Lazarus has already died. Nevertheless, the disciples agree to go with Jesus. By the time they reach Lazarus' home, he has been dead and buried four days.

Martha and then Mary followed by the mourners meet Jesus on the road. Both women profess their belief in him as the Messiah and the resurrection of the dead. Jesus weeps with them. Then he asks them where they placed Lazarus' body. When they show him the cave with a stone lying against it, Jesus orders men to remove the stone. Martha doesn't want the stone removed because a body decays rapidly in a hot climate causing a terrible stench. Nevertheless, Jesus orders the stone removed. Then he orders Lazarus to come out of the tomb and for men to unbind the strips of cloth on his face and body. People are amazed. Lazarus is resurrected and restored to health simply by Jesus' voice command.

What is the religious significance of this miracle?

Mary: I believe just as God created the world through voice command, Jesus brought Lazarus back to life by voice command. Also, God's kingdom is actively present in and through Jesus' ministry. He gives us new life.

Milton: Jesus has power over life and death. He frees us from other kinds of tombs, too, such as the meaningless tombs of anger, resentments, hatred, jealousies, selfishness, and self-centeredness that hold us.

And this event prefigures or foreshadows Jesus' own death and resurrection.

Anita: Yes, you are right. This miracle is viewed as a serious challenge by Temple authorities. Some Jews who witnessed this miracle go to the Pharisees and tell them what happened.

> So the chief priests and Pharisees called a meeting of the council, and said, "What are we to do? This man is performing many signs. If we let him go on like this, everyone will believe in him, and the Romans will come and destroy both our holy place and our nation." But one of them, Caiaphas, who was high priest that year, said to them, "You know nothing at all! You do not understand that it is better for you to have one man die for the people than to have the whole nation destroyed." He did not say this on his own, but being high priest that year he prophesied that Jesus was about to die for the nation, and not for the nation only, but to gather into one the dispersed children of God. So from that day on they planned to put him to death.[31]

Caiaphas' prophesy becomes true not only regarding the death of Jesus to keep political and religious order and control over the people but also for the redemption of all believers.

Let me conclude with "The Legend of St. Valentine." It goes as follows.

***

Many, many years ago and long after Jesus was crucified by Roman soldiers, Roman Emperor Claudius II ordered all people to worship 12 Roman gods. Christians refused to worship false gods. They were faithful followers of Jesus and worshipped only God.

A Christian by the name of Valentinus was arrested, imprisoned, and sentenced to death because he would not worship the Roman gods. His jailer was a good man who had a daughter who was born blind. His jailer asked a favor of Valentinus. He said, "I see that you are a man of learning and know many things. My wife and I have a beautiful daughter who was born blind. Could you, would you teach her some of the things you know?"

Valentinus replied, "I will be glad to share with her what little knowledge I have. Bring her to me."

Soon Valentinus was teaching Julia, the jailer's daughter, about nature, mathematics, and God. Julia was a good and eager student. She trusted Valentinus and believed in everything he taught her. She saw the world through his eyes and his love for her. Through Valentinus, light entered Julia's eyes.

One day Julia asked him, "Valentinus, does God answer prayer?"

Valentinus answered, "God hears every prayer but may not answer every prayer the way people want their prayers answered."

"I pray every day that God will let me see the world you describe to me. Do you think I will ever be able to see?" she asked.

Valentinus answered, "God does what is best for us. We must believe in God and accept God's decision."

The two of them knelt and prayed in his prison cell. They were quiet a long time. Suddenly Julia cried out, "I can see. Valentinus! I can see. God has heard my prayer and says 'Yes.'"

They both praised God and thanked God for the gift of sight.

Not too many days later Valentinus was executed on February 14, 270 CE for his belief in Jesus as God's Messiah and chosen one. The night before Valentinus' execution, he wrote Julia a letter urging her always to pray and to stay close to God and to follow the teachings of Jesus.

Julia planted a pink blossomed almond tree near his grave. Ever since, the almond tree has become a symbol of love and friendship in the Lord.

Think About It

- Do you believe in miracles?
- Do you believe God intervenes in our world?
- Should we expect miracles today from God?
- What role in miracles do we play?

Chapter 7

Understanding Jesus' Parables, Part I

The kingdom of God is as if someone would scatter seed on the ground, and would sleep and rise night and day, and the seed would sprout and grow, he does not know how. The earth produces of itself, first the stalk, then the head, then the full grain in the head. But when the grain is ripe, at once he goes in with his sickle, because the harvest has come.

With what can we compare the kingdom of God, or what parable will we use for it? It is like a mustard seed, which, when sown upon the ground is the smallest of all the seeds on earth; yet when it is sown it grows up and becomes the greatest of all shrubs, and puts forth large branches, so that the birds of the air can make nests in its shade.

Mark 4:26-32

Anita: There is no simple description for parables. They are open-ended earthly stories that indirectly teach a spiritual truth. Jesus used parables as the opposition to his ministry increased. By using them, Jesus could reveal spiritual truths to the receptive and hide them from the non-receptive listener. Parables challenge accepted norms and open the listener to new insights and truths.

In the parables of the unseen growth of seeds and the mustard seed, God reigns. The seeds, no matter how small, come from God. They take root and blossom. They possess the secret of life and growth. Farmers plant and wait patiently, hopefully, and ready for the harvest.

Thomas: Do these parables mean that faith grows unseen similar to the mustard seed?

Anita: Yes.

Thomas: But not all seed is good seed. Bad seed exists amongst the good seed and often chokes the spiritual and physical life out of the good seed. Then what?

Anita: Your question plagues us all. Jesus addresses this very question in his parable of the wheat and tares. The parable goes as follows:

> The kingdom of heaven is like a man who sowed good seed in his field. But while everyone was sleeping, his enemy came and sowed weeds among the wheat, and went away. When the wheat sprouted and formed heads, then the weeds also appeared.
>
> The owner's servants came to him and said, 'Sir, didn't you sow good seed in your field? Where then did the weeds come from?'
>
> 'An enemy did this,' he replied.
>
> The servants asked him, 'Do you want us to go and pull them up?'
>
> 'No,' he answered, 'because while you are pulling the weeds, you may root up the wheat with them. Let both grow together until the harvest. At that time I will tell the harvesters:

> First collect the weeds and tie them in bundles to be burned; then gather the wheat and bring it into my barn.'[32]

Thomas: So, if you are considered a weed or an enemy, you will eventually be separated and thrown into the fire.

Anita: Yes. Jesus explained in private to his disciples that the weeds are the sons of the devil. He says:

> The one who sows the good seed is the Son of Man; the field is the world, and the good seed are the children of the kingdom; the weeds are the children of the evil one, and the enemy who sowed them is the devil; the harvest is the end of the age, and the reapers are angels. Just as the weeds are collected and burned up with fire, so will it be at the end of the age.[33]

This parable always troubled me until I read a good explanation of the tares. They are a weed known as bearded darnel and are a wheat look alike and impossible to distinguish from wheat in their early stages of growth. The roots of the tares intertwine with the roots of the wheat making it impossible to separate them without destroying both plants. Also the darnel is slightly poisonous. So what do you think the spiritual truth may be for this parable?

Mary: God allows evil to exist alongside good until harvest time which, I assume, will be at our death.

Milton: God's judgment and justice will occur sooner or later. In the meantime, we should not allow ourselves to be seduced or choked by the growth of the bad seed. I would like to think there is always time for repentance and God's acceptance of sinners.

Thomas: Could this parable be a warning not to judge others. Bad seeds or people often can masquerade as good seeds or people. Perhaps in the end God alone is the judge.

Mary: Also, people who seem undesirable to us could actually be secretly very good. Sinners, too, often make a U-turn to redeem themselves and others.

Anita: Very good. I like what you all said. It is important not to judge people as God is the ultimate judge. And God always keeps the door open until judgment day.

Are there any parables that trouble you and/or are helpful to you that you would like to discuss?

Thomas: I hear from my girlfriend and her family the importance of the Christian faith. They often tell me verbatim the pearl of great price. "The kingdom of heaven is like a merchant in search of fine pearls; on finding one pearl of great value, he went and sold all that he had and bought it."[34] They expect me to do likewise. They want me to leave everybody I know and let them and their church become my entire world. If I want to marry their daughter, I must first join their church. In fact, they are very upset that she and I watched on TV Pope Francis at Madison Square Garden.

Anita: Do you or your girlfriend feel intimidated? Are you and she afraid of them?

Thomas: I fear harm may come to her if I don't do what they say. And I believe some of their church members are stalking us.

Milton: Do you think they are a cult? And who is their leader? What is he like?

Thomas: They may be a cult. But don't most cults keep women from getting an education? She is studying to become a doctor. That's why I think they may not be a cult.

Milton: Does she live at home? What's her mother's relationship to her father?

Thomas: She lives at home. Her mother seems devoted to her father and does whatever he asks her to do. The same applies to my girlfriend.

Anita: Have you ever asked her if her family belongs to a cult and why they put so much pressure on you to join them?

Thomas: Yes, I have. She says they do not belong to a cult, that they are a close-knit faith community that has found the pearl of great value. She believes there is nothing sinister about their beliefs.

Anita: What do your parents and friends say about your situation with your girlfriend and her family?

Thomas: They like her but think she is too much under the influence of her family and church. That's why I am here. As you know, I come from a non-religious family and want to learn from you. Does the Christian religion and Jesus' parable of the pearl of great value give them the right to coerce me into their way of believing?

Anita: Absolutely not. Since you make a good living, have they ever asked you to support their church?

Thomas: Yes, all the time. And I am not even a member.

Anita: Do you attend worship with her? If so, what is it like?

Thomas: No. I am not allowed in their church until I become a member. So, I don't know what goes on.

Anita: That's unusual. Churches have open doors and all are welcomed.

Sarah: As you know Thomas, I am a psychologist and the mother of a daughter who has married outside of my Jewish faith. She is married to a Christian and has a little girl and boy. To my knowledge, her experiences with Christians have been positive and there has been no coercion. Something is not right with your situation. Here is my business card. Come see me as soon as possible; and if you want, bring your girlfriend. There will be no charge. In the meantime, learn what you can from the people gathered here. They mean well.

Anita: Thank you Sarah. I hope you can help Thomas bring clarity to his situation. And I agree, Thomas, you should meet with her soon.

I believe the spiritual truth of the pearl of great value is that the rewards in the kingdom of heaven surpass all material things and are worth the price paid. It is the cost of discipleship. In the Lord's Prayer, we pray, "Thy kingdom come, thy will be done on earth as it is in heaven." Remember we discussed the Kingdom of God is a spiritual kingdom where God's universal rule reigns. It is an era of peace and righteousness that transforms society as well as the individual. Those who accept Jesus and his message work to bring in this kingdom. Jesus cautions us to beware of some leaders' sense of self-importance and the spiritual power they claim is theirs and the distorted beliefs they teach. He calls them wolves in sheep's clothes.

Edward: What I don't like about this parable of the pearl of great value is its self-centeredness bordering on selfishness. In essence it says, "I am saved and the rest of you are damned." I wonder whether Jesus even said this parable especially since it is not about service, self-giving, love, charity, and living according to Jesus' teachings.

Anita: Well said. I agree with you. It is interesting to note that this parable only appears in Matthew and not the other three gospels. I wonder what was going through the mind of the author of this gospel when he wrote this parable and put these words into Jesus' mouth. Faith, not fear, is what needs to take root in us.

Edward: Related to the parable of the pearl, can we ferret out the spiritual truth in the parable of the Good Samaritan?[35] We could endanger our safety if we stop to help someone along the roadside. It could be a ruse used to attack us.

Anita: There is always that danger. But I think Jesus was responding to the lawyer who questions Jesus what he must do to inherit eternal life. Jesus asks him what is written in the Law. The lawyer answers, "You shall love the Lord your God with all your heart, with all your soul, with all your strength, and with all your mind; and your neighbor as yourself."[36] This saying is known as the great love commandment.

In this exchange between Jesus and the lawyer who wants to justify himself regarding his excellent adherence to the Law, he asks Jesus who is my neighbor? Jesus replies with the parable of the Good Samaritan.

> A man was going down from Jerusalem to Jericho, and fell into the hands of robbers, who stripped him, beat him, and went away, leaving him half dead. Now by chance a priest was going down that road; and when he saw him, he passed by on the other side. So likewise, a Levite, when he came to the place and saw him, passed by on the other side. But a Samaritan while traveling came near him; and when he saw him, he was moved with pity. He went to him and bandaged his wounds, having poured oil and wine on them. Then he put him on his own animal, brought him to an inn, and took care of him. The next day he took out two denarii, gave them to the innkeeper, and said, 'Take care of him; and when I

> come back, I will repay you whatever more you spend.' Which of these three, do you think, was a neighbor to the man who fell into the hands of the robbers? He said, 'The one who showed him mercy.' Jesus said to him, 'go and do likewise.'[37]

Milton: Jesus tells us that our neighbor is the person in need even if he is not part of our tribe or religious community. The great love commandment and its accompanying compassion take precedence over the Law. Also, the reward of eternal life should not be our reason to help the needy. Compassion and love alone should motivate us.

Anita: You are referring to agape love or selfless/self-sacrificing love.

A thrilling fictitious story entitled *Nathan's Run* by John Gilstrap illustrates the observance of the Law at the expense of the great love commandment. A shortened summary of part of this story goes as follows.

Nathan Bailey is orphaned at age 10. His mother died shortly after his birth. Upon the accidental death of his attorney father, the court assigns Nathan to the care and custody of his alcoholic, ex-convict uncle, Mark Bailey. Nathan's father's friends plead Nathan's cause in the courts and with juvenile authorities not to let him be placed in the care and custody of his uncle but to no avail.

Nathan's uncle and friends abuse him emotionally, psychologically, and physically. Nathan learned to drive a truck on his deceased grandfather's farm. In desperation, Nathan decides to steal his uncle's truck and run away. He is caught. His uncle presses charges. At age 11, Nathan is sentenced to a Virginia juvenile detention center where he is the youngest detainee. The other youth in this detention center continuously attack him and steal his food.

On the fourth of July, a guard drags him by the ear from the recreational center for some unknown offense and puts him in an isolated cell. He removes Nathan's shoes and takes them with him. A few hours later the guard returns drunk.

He opens Nathan's cell, takes out a knife, and attempts to kill the unarmed Nathan. A struggle follows. Nathan has the advantage of alertness and agility. His attacker has the advantage of size, surprise, and a knife. Nathan dodges his attacker and escapes his first blow. Nathan sinks his teeth into the guard's hand and the knife drops to the floor. Nathan grabs the knife and kills the guard. Nathan didn't mean to kill the guard and keeps saying, "I'm sorry!"

Nathan takes the guard's keys and escapes from the detention center. He has no plan and no place to go. He breaks into an unoccupied home to get cleaned up, to rest, and to get something to eat.

Nathan turns on the TV and radio. He learns that politicians and policemen are enraged that one of their own has been killed in the line of duty. They want to capture Nathan and sentence him to death. Nathan calls a national radio talk show hostess, Denise Carpenter, to tell his side of the story. His voice and his honest, frank recounting of the events leading to his killing of his guard causes Denise and others to suspect that Nathan may be telling the truth.

Nathan is afraid to turn himself in because he believes the police will kill him. He decides to take the owner's BMW and go to Canada once nighttime falls. He has no money, does not dare to stop for gas, and can only go as far as a tank of gasoline will take him. He reaches southern New York State.

Eventually Nathan is captured, brutally treated by the New York police, and put in solitary confinement. A crime boss' hit man, dressed as a policeman, enters the jail, kills two policemen on duty and makes it look as though Nathan murdered both policemen.

No one questions where Nathan would get a gun unless he had an accomplice. Nathan heard the hit man's gun, equipped with a silencer, kill the first policeman. He takes the broken bed stand leg in his cell and with it knocks the killer's gun from his hand when he enters his cell. The hit man struggles some more. Nathan cracks the stunned hit man a couple of more times with the bed stand leg and leaves. The hit man leaves and takes with him the video tapes that record his murders. Nathan is blamed as the killer of the two policemen.

Again Nathan escapes with nowhere to go. The hit man leaves the jail and searches in the vicinity for Nathan. The local sheriff gives the green light to the police to shoot Nathan on sight.

Nathan hides in a dilapidated apartment house basement. A 10-year old black boy, Billy, happens upon Nathan in the basement. Billy recognizes Nathan from TV. Nathan asks him to listen to his side of the story and to hide him. Billy believes Nathan's story and takes him to his apartment. Nathan calls Denise and tells her that the cops are out to kill him.

Virginia Detective Michaels interrupts Denise's program and asks to speak to Nathan. She is outraged that he is barging in on her show. Detective Michaels believes everyone has been looking at the evidence in the wrong way. Upon his examination of the three dead policemen, Michaels believes that there is a contract out to kill Nathan and that Nathan's life is in danger. Denise lets Detective Michaels speak to Nathan off the air waves. The detective pleads with Nathan to trust him, to get away from Billy's place before he is killed, and to meet him in the town square.

***

How does this story illustrate Jesus' message in the Good Samaritan parable?

Mary: You may say that initially Nathan had been abandoned by the courts and child's services. Nathan's father's friends allowed themselves to be defeated in his defense by the court system. Nathan is a helpless victim of a miscarriage of justice. He is thrown into the ditch of unwanted humanity with his abusive uncle and his friends.

Sarah: Not only that, why does his uncle press charges against Nathan for stealing his truck? What motivates his uncle? Is there an inheritance he wants to claim for himself? Is he paying the hit man? And where are the juvenile detention supervisors that they allow a guard to isolate this child and to get drunk on duty? Was the guard or guards in the pay of Nathan's uncle?

Edward: Other than for Billy, TV host Denise Carpenter, and Detective Michaels, evil has the upper hand in this story. So far in this story, Billy is the only Good Samaritan who risks possible death to rescue a helpless, innocent victim. Fear and hopelessness stalk Nathan. Yet he doesn't give up.

Milton: I agree. Nathan had no safe sanctuary and no friends. You could say his nightmare is similar to the Syrian refugee crisis and their need for sanctuary. Pieter Bruegel in 1560 did an engraving entitled *Justice.* In it, Lady Justice is blindfolded. She stands in the midst of human cruelty and does nothing. Yet people are hung from the gallows, tied to a post and whipped, tied to bodily stretching racks and all sorts of other cruelties. Nathan has been wronged by uncle, society, the judicial system and juvenile authorities, inmates in the detention center, and opportunistic police and politicians.

Sarah: As this story illustrates, it is dangerous for society to accept as true unfounded opinions on a crime when these opinions may openly reflect someone's poor thinking, narrow mindedness, or opportunism.

Anita: Also, cruelty, taking advantage of the vulnerable, and ignoring those people who need our help violate the great love commandment and is unacceptable to Jesus.

Thomas: You have given me a lot to think about. I will try not to judge others so quickly but will ask myself who lives according to the great love commandment. And how can I be a Good Samaritan?

Think About It

- How are all the parables discussed today connected?
- Did you gain any new insights?
- Can you think of ways love can govern the little miracles of life?
- How does *Nathan's Run* affect you?
- What would you do if given an opportunity to help Nathan as he flees the policemen and hitman?

Chapter 8

Understanding Jesus' Parables, Part II

To-morrow, and to-morrow, and to-morrow,
Creeps in this petty pace from day to day,
To the last syllable of recorded time;
And all our yesterdays have lighted fools
The way to dusty death. Out, out, brief candle!
Life's but a walking shadow, a poor player,
That struts and frets his hour upon the stage,
And then is heard no more....

Macbeth
William Shakespeare

Anita: Today, let us consider how Jesus' parables help us set our GPS for our life's voyage on the high seas of life or whether we allow ourselves to remain stuck circling a bobbing bell buoy.

You may find the parable of the Rich Man known as Dives and Lazarus informative and instructive. It is a folk-tale that originated in Egypt. Jesus adapts it to his time and speaks about missed opportunities and incorrect religious belief. This parable by Jesus is found in Luke 16:19-31. Let me read it to all of you.

> There was a rich man who was dressed in purple and fine linen and who feasted sumptuously every day. And at his

> gate lay a poor man named Lazarus, covered with sores, who longed to satisfy his hunger with what fell from the rich man's table; even the dogs would come and lick his sores. The poor man died and was carried away by the angels to be with Abraham. The rich man also died and was buried. In Hades, where he was being tormented, he looked up and saw Abraham far away with Lazarus by his side. He called out, 'Father Abraham, have mercy on me, and send Lazarus to dip the tip of his finger in water and cool my tongue; for I am in agony in these flames.' But Abraham said, 'Child, remember that during your lifetime you received your good things, and Lazarus in like manner evil things; but now he is comforted here, and you are in agony. Besides all this, between you and us a great chasm has been fixed, so that those who might want to pass from here to you cannot do so, and no one can cross from there to us.' He said, 'Then, father, I beg you to send him to my father's house—for I have five brothers—that he may warn them, so that they will not also come into this place of torment.' Abraham replied, 'They have Moses and the prophets; they should listen to them.' He said, 'No father Abraham; but if someone goes to them from the dead, they will repent.' He said to him, 'If they do not listen to Moses and the prophets, neither will they be convinced even if someone rises from the dead.'

What is the spiritual truth in this parable?

Milton: The rich man lived a life of self-indulgence. All his material needs were met while Lazarus at his door lives in abject poverty. Dives does not take any interest in this poor man. Yet he knows Lazarus by name. He knows that he exists. And as a

Sadducee, he doesn't believe in a judgment day and an afterlife. At death, the roles and eternal destiny of the two men are reversed. Dives is in torment and Lazarus sits at the heavenly banquet table.

Thomas: Is Jesus proposing here a doctrine of rewards and punishment?

Anita: I think so. But he is also pointing a finger at Dives' moral indifference and the missed opportunities given to him. He failed to use his wealth properly while alive. He should have used it to improve the lives of the needy. He lived as though the present moment and his self-indulgences are the summation of life. To him there is no Judgment Day and afterlife.

Thomas: Even though Dives sees Lazarus at Abraham's banquet table, he still assumes his earthly sense of superiority. He wants Lazarus to be his lackey and fetch him some water.

Milton: Also, Dives claims his tormented condition is a result of his lack of knowledge about an afterlife. Therefore, he wants Lazarus to warn his brothers.

Mary: I like Abraham's response to Dives. There is no excuse for his lack of knowledge. He had the prophets and scripture to instruct him about his earthly conduct upon which hang the issues of eternal life and death. Dives' thoughts and actions were limited only to himself and the paradise he created for himself.

Anita: Jesus told this parable for the benefit of the Pharisees and Sadducees who enjoy their wealth and believe their wealth is a sign of God's pleasure. They believe the wretched poor are a sign of God's displeasure. With this parable, Jesus refutes these assumptions.

Sarah: The Law of Moses mandates people share their wealth with the poor. It says: "You shall open wide your hand to your brother, to the needy, and to the poor, in the land."[38] Those people who have plenty to eat, but will not share their food with the hungry, cannot enter God's kingdom. The "Bus Stop" story you told us a while back emphasizes this point too.

Anita: This parable also prefigures Jesus' resurrection and those who do not believe in him. Jesus insists in this parable that he, and not the self-satisfied and well-fed Pharisees and Sadducees, provides the correct spiritual direction for people's lives. What types of sins are exhibited in this parable?

Mary: Sins of the spirit, omission, and moral indifference. This parable also reminds me of the parable of the tax collector and Pharisee. Can we discuss it now?

Anita: Yes. Jesus tells us that

> Two men went up to the temple to pray, one a Pharisee and the other a tax collector. The Pharisee, standing by himself, was praying thus, 'God I thank you that I am not like other people: thieves, rogues, adulterers, or even like this tax collector. I fast twice a week; I give a tenth of all my income.' But the tax collector, standing far off, would not even look up to heaven, but was beating his breast and saying, 'God, be merciful to me, a sinner!' I tell you, this man went down to his home justified rather than the other; for all who exalt themselves will be humbled, but all who humble themselves will be exalted.[39]

Why did Jesus say this?

Mary: The Pharisee is really not in communication with God. He tells God what a righteous person he is and wants God to ratify his sense of self-worth. He goes so far as to single out for comparison the tax collector whom he does not even know, let alone what may be in his contrite heart.

Sarah: The Pharisee exhibits spiritual pride with his emphasis on how he fulfills Jewish legal observances. What we have here is outward conformity versus inner motives and a violation of the great love commandment.

Milton: I believe Jesus tells us that God does not accept those who in their pride and sense of self-righteousness parade their assumed moral virtue while the tax collector's body language shows humility and contrition. He understands the dynamic character of God's reign and God's ultimate gracious character. The tax collector makes no claim to any rights before God. He stands bankrupt before God and casts himself on God's compassion and mercy.

Anita: Yes, the tax collector is honest with himself. He has no grand illusions. He stands in humility, genuineness, and sincerity before God.

Thomas: In other words, you can't play games with God. You can't make a claim on God and parade your self-righteousness as a virtue that God must accept.

Anita: Yes. Along those lines, Jesus has several parables about people who are lost and then found. He speaks of God's love for all of us and how God seeks out even the foolish lost sheep and leaves 99 sheep in the wilderness until he finds the lost sheep. Then Jesus says:

> 'Rejoice with me for I have found my sheep that was lost.' Just so, I tell you, there will be more joy in heaven over one sinner

> who repents than over ninety-nine righteous persons who need no repentance.[40]

Thomas: That doesn't seem fair. Other than for monetary consideration, if the sheep wanders off, why should the shepherd leave the other sheep in danger's way to find the lost one?

Anita: In Jesus' time, sheep were owned by villages. Two or three shepherds were in charge of a flock so that one shepherd could leave the sheep in the care of the other shepherds. One shepherd would then search for the lost sheep. Maybe the sheep could not find its way back to the flock without the help of the seeking shepherd who, in this parable, represents God.

Thomas: Oh!

Anita: Thomas, you raised a very legitimate question a lot of people have. It is more pronounced in the parable of the Prodigal Son. The word *prodigal* when used as an adjective means lavish and wasteful. When we speak of a prodigal son, we mean a son who was extremely lavish and wasteful.

To many people, this parable seems so unfair to the good, responsible son. Let's take a closer look at it.

> There was a man who had two sons. The younger of them said to his father, 'Father, give me the share of the property that will belong to me.' So he divided his property between them. A few days later the younger son gathered all he had and traveled to a distant country, and there he squandered his property in dissolute living. When he had spent everything, a severe famine took place throughout that country, and he began to be in need. So he went and hired himself out to one of the citizens of that country, who sent him to his fields to feed the pigs. He would gladly have filled himself with the pods that the pigs

> were eating; and no one gave him anything. But when he came to himself he said, 'How many of my father's hired hands have bread enough and to spare, but here I am dying of hunger! I will get up and go to my father, and I will say to him, "Father, I have sinned against heaven and before you; I am no longer worthy to be called your son; treat me like one of your hired hands."' So he set off and went to his father. But while he was still far off, his father saw him and was filled with compassion; he ran and put his arms around him and kissed him. Then the son said to him, 'Father, I have sinned against heaven and before you; I am no longer worthy to be called your son.' But the father said to his slaves, 'Quickly, bring out a robe—the best one—and put it on him; put a ring on his finger and sandals on his feet. And get the fatted calf and kill it, and let us eat and celebrate; for this son of mine was dead and is alive again; he was lost and is found!' And they began to celebrate.[41]

Sarah: Thomas you need to know that Jewish custom allotted two-thirds of a father's estate to the oldest son, and only one-third to the younger son. Estates were usually divided upon the death of the father. To live with swine is to live outside the Jewish people's covenant with God. The pods referred to in the parable were carob pods. Animals ate them, and sometimes even desperately poor people ate them.

Milton: I assume the father represents God. The father gave both sons freedom to make their own choices, good or bad.

Mary: In other words, we make our own choices that determine our future. Nothing is predetermined.

Anita: Yes. The father forgives the wayward son and restores him to the family. But this welcome home celebration offends his eldest son. In his anger, he tells his father:

> 'Listen! For all these years I have been working like a slave for you, and I have never disobeyed your command; yet you have never given me even a young goat so that I might celebrate with my friends. But when this son of yours came back, who has devoured your property with prostitutes; you killed the fatted calf for him!' Then the father said to him, 'Son, you are always with me, and all that is mine is yours. But we had to celebrate and rejoice, because this brother of yours was dead and has come to life; he was lost and have been found.[42]

You see, the father is sympathetic and loving toward both sons. God loves us unconditionally. The father has great capacity for love, forgiveness, mercy, compassion, and grace towards both sons.

Thomas: Are we then expected to forgive those who wrong us? Suppose someone is unrepentant? Is it fair that God is happier over the repentance of a sinner than over the behavior of good people? Don't the lost create many of the problems in this world?

Anita: You have a lot of questions. Do you think the Prodigal Son was repentant?

Thomas: Yes. He was. It must have been humiliating for him to return home and admit his wrong doing. He was not asking his father to restore him to the family. He was asking to be made one of his father's hired hands. Nothing else.

Anita: In this parable, there are two lost sons—one who went to a foreign country and squandered his inheritance, the other who lived behind a barricade of self-righteousness and self-imposed slavery to his father. Both were selfish in their own way. We are not told whether the two brothers ever reconciled. Jesus left that decision to his hearers. He entreated them to rejoice and celebrate over the restoration of a sinner.

An adaptation of Henry Van Dyke's parable of *The Happy Prince* illustrates the essence of what Jesus tries to teach us through some of his parables. The story goes as follows.

***

Once, long ago in a faraway land at a time when birds could talk and magic still was possible, there stood on a hill high above a city a statue called the Happy Prince. He was painted all over with gold leaf; and for eyes, he had two precious jewels called sapphires which glittered with a bright light. He held a gold sword with a brilliant ruby of great value in his hilt.

Everyone in the city looked up at the statue and admired it, each in his own way. The important men who were friends of the mayor spoke of the statue as a work of art, although not useful in any practical way.

One night when it was nearly winter, a tiny bird called a swallow flew over that city on his way to Egypt. He grew tired and looked for a place to sleep. He saw the golden statue of the Happy Prince and landed just between the statue's feet. "I will spend the night in this golden bedroom," he said, and put his head under his wing and tried to go to sleep. Suddenly he felt a large drop of water fall on his head.

"Is it raining?" He asked. "How can it be? The stars are out and there are no clouds in the sky. I can see by the light of the moon."

Then another drop fell, and then another. "I must find a barn or someplace where I can be dry," he said to himself. But as he started to fly away, he looked up and saw where the drops were coming from.

They were tears! The statue of the Happy Prince was crying! The little bird flew up to his shoulder and saw the teardrops running down the Happy Prince's golden cheeks, which were glistening in the moonlight.

"Why are you crying?" the little swallow asked. "And who are you, anyway?"

"I am called the Happy Prince," the statue answered.

"Well, if you're the Happy Prince, then why are you crying?"

"When I was alive, I had a human heart; and I lived in a palace where there were no tears and there was no sadness. There was nothing to do but play all day and dance all night inside the walls of the palace. I never saw anything outside those walls; and inside them, everything was beautiful. And I was called the Happy Prince, because happiness is the only thing that I ever knew.

"But now that I am dead, they have made a statue of me and put me up so high that I can see the whole city, where there is so much trouble and so much unhappiness that I can only weep.

"Way down in the town on a crooked street there is a falling-down house with a leaking roof and an open window. I can see a poor woman who makes her living sewing for other people. Her hands are pricked by needles and pins, and her eyes are weary from trying to make perfect stitches. She is embroidering passion flowers on a ball gown for one of the Queen's maids of honor. She must keep sewing, for she is poor; but she is also watching over her sick little boy who lies in a corner of the room with a high fever. He is thirsty, and he is crying for orange juice. She has no money for oranges or for a doctor.

"Little swallow, please take the ruby from my sword and carry it down to her. My golden feet are anchored in stone and I cannot go myself."

The swallow dug the big red ruby from the golden sword and put it in his beak. He flew over the city, pass the great cathedral with the marble angels and pass the palace where the Happy Prince once lived. He crossed the river and saw the lights from the ships in the harbor. He flew over the marketplace where people were bargaining over things to buy and sell and into the section where the poor people lived.

Finally he came to the house where the woman fretted over her feverish son. She dozed for a moment, exhausted by her sewing and her worrying. The bird put the jewel on the table by her embroidery thread, and fluttered around the boy's bed, cooling his fever with the fanning of his wings.

The child awoke, feeling the soothing breeze, said, "Mama, I feel better now. I think I am going to get well." Then he fell into a gentle sleep.

When the swallow returned to the Happy Prince, he said to the statue, "Even though winter is near, I feel warm. I wonder why?"

"You have done something for someone else. That is why you feel warm."

The next day the swallow bid his friend goodbye.

"Please little swallow, do not leave yet! Please stay one more night."

"But all my friends are waiting for me. They are seeing the great stone statues of Egypt and the Pyramids, and the fierce lions that come to the Nile to drink. There is warmth there, and much to see.

"Oh little swallow, down another street in a tall narrow house, there sits a young man in a cold attic with no heat and no food. Yet he is fired with dreams of writing a play for the theater. But he is too cold and hungry to write anymore."

I will stay with you only one more night. Do you have another ruby to send?"

"I have no more rubies," the Happy Prince replied. "I only have the sapphires that are my eyes. Take one of them to the young man so that he may sell it to buy food and firewood."

"But I cannot pluck out your eye!" the little swallow said as he began to cry.

"Please, please, little swallow. Do as I ask." The little swallow took the sapphire from the Happy Prince's eye, and flew with it to the young man's attic. He entered through a hole in the roof and found the young man so discouraged that he had his head on his desk weeping. He did not see the swallow or hear the beating of his wings. When he looked up, he found the brilliant jewel on his desk and laughed with joy, because now he could afford to finish his play.

On his way back, the swallow flew by the boats in the harbor and watched the sailors load the cargo in preparation for their voyage south.

"I'll be leaving on my way to Egypt," the swallow said to himself, and he flew back to tell the Happy Prince farewell.

"Oh please, little swallow stay one more night with me," the statue begged.

"But it is almost winter and soon there will be snow and ice."

"Little swallow, listen to me. In the marketplace below there is a little girl who sells matches. She has no shoes and no coat, and she is cold. She has dropped her matches in the water, and they are ruined. She is afraid to go home for fear her father will beat her for dropping them. She is crying, because they have no money. Take my other eye and give it to her so her father will not punish her."

"I will stay with you one more night, but I cannot take your other eye. Then you would be blind."

"Please, please, little swallow. Do as I ask."

The swallow plucked out the last jewel the Happy Prince possessed, and flew it down to the little girl below. She laughed with joy when she received the brilliant blue stone and ran home to show her father.

The little bird flew back to the Happy Prince. "Because you are blind now, I will stay with you and be your eyes." He shivered as he settled down under the fold of his wing at the Prince's feet.

"No, little swallow. Now you must go to Egypt."

But the little bird refused to go; and all day he sat on the statue's shoulder and told him of all the marvelous things he had seen in his travels through many lands, of the great white birds who stand on long legs on the banks of the Nile and spear the fish with their beaks, and of the great stone Sphinx who keeps watch over the Pyramids and watches over the desert sands.

But the statue was troubled and said, "Although you tell of many wondrous things in faraway lands, there is sadness in this great city. Fly over my city and tell me what you see."

The little swallow flew over the city; and he saw rich people in their great houses, while outside their walls were beggars at the gates. Close by were dark lanes where hungry children peered through dirty windows dreaming of the summer. Under the arch of a stone bridge, he saw two small boys huddling together to keep warm. They were starving, because they had no food to eat. An angry watchman, not caring for anyone but himself, chased them from their shelter out into the rain.

The swallow told the Happy Prince all that he had seen.

"Please little swallow, peel off my gold covering, flake by flake and give it to the people who are suffering."

So the little bird flaked off the gold paint, little by little, and gave it to the poor so they could buy bread. Finally the Happy Prince was no longer golden, but a dingy leaden grey.

The snow came along, with sleet and frost. Icicles hung from the houses; their sharp points glistened in the sun. The poor little swallow shivered and grew colder, but he would not leave the prince he had come to love so dearly. He tried to keep alive by living on crumbs he found outside a nearby bakery, and he flapped his wings to stay warm.

Finally he knew he was becoming weaker and weaker, and that he was going to die. He flew up to the Prince's shoulder in one last grand effort, to say goodbye.

"It is time you were going to Egypt," the statue said, thinking that was what the swallow meant. "You have stayed with me far too long. Kiss me on the lips to say goodbye, for you know that I love you."

"I am not going to Egypt," the swallow said. "I am going to die."

And as he kissed the Prince, he fell dead at the statue's feet.

Was it the frost or was it heartbreak? No one knows. But just as the swallow died, there was a loud crack inside the statue, and the leaden heart of the Happy Prince broke in two.

The next day the mayor and his important friends walked through the square and looked up at the statue of the Happy Prince, no longer beautiful and golden, but dull and shabby grey.

"We must pull it down and burn it!" he said. "We will replace it with a statue of me."

"Why you?" one of his important followers asked. "Why not me?"

"You?" another echoed. "Why not me?"

And they argued and they argued, and may still be arguing.

The man who tried to burn the statue of the Happy Prince in a fiery furnace found that no matter how hot the flame or how many coals he heaped on the fire, the leaden heart would not melt. So he threw it on a scrap heap alongside the body of the tiny dead swallow.

God looked down from heaven and asked an angel to bring to God the two most precious things in the whole city. Instead of any jewels or gold, the angel brought back the heart of lead and the little dead bird.

"You have chosen well," God said.

***

Think About It

- Why do you think God thought the angel chose well?
- Do you believe in second chances? Why or why not?
- If given a second chance in life, how would you use it?
- Have you experienced what it is like to do something kind and good for someone else? What did it feel like?
- How have the Happy Prince and the swallow taken on Jesus-like qualities?
- In what ways are the Prodigal Son and the Happy Prince similar yet different?
- In what ways are Dives and the prodigal's elder brother similar yet different?
- Where do you place yourself in Jesus' parables and in *The Happy Prince*?
- Did any of today's characters set for himself a GPS destination? What happened?
- What did you learn today about God?

Chapter 9

Jesus—A Man of Sorrows

> *Men never do evil so completely and cheerfully as when they do it from religious conviction.*
>
> *Pensees*
> Blaise Pascal

Anita: The Synoptic Gospels of Matthew, Mark, and Luke suggest that the grown Jesus entered Jerusalem for the first time on Palm Sunday. The Gospel of John indicates that many of the events that happened during Holy Week occurred at an earlier time.

Jesus turns from teaching in the countryside and decides to go to Jerusalem to teach in the Temple. By doing so, he enters Herod's territory and will put himself in harm's way. Even some Pharisees warn him to:

> "Get away from here, for Herod wants to kill you." He said to them, "Go and tell that fox for me, 'Listen, I am casting out demons and performing cures today and tomorrow, and on the third day I finish my work. Yet today, tomorrow, and the next day I must be on my way, because it is impossible for a prophet to be killed outside of Jerusalem.' Jerusalem, Jerusalem, the city that kills the prophets and stones those

> who are sent to it! How often have I desired to gather your children together as a hen gathers her brood under wings, and you were not willing![43]

Thomas: Does Jesus have a death wish?

Anita: No. I don't think so. He knows his time is limited before he will be assassinated. So why not face the political/religious establishment head on? He is discouraged because even his disciples fail to understand who he is and what his mission is. On his approach to Caesarea Philippi, he asks his disciples:

> 'Who do people say that I am?' And they answered him, "John the Baptist, and others, Elijah; and still others, one of the prophets." He asked them, "But who do you say that I am?" Peter answered him, "You are the Messiah." And he sternly ordered them not to tell anyone about him.[44]

Thomas: Why doesn't he want anyone to know he is the Messiah?

Anita: Jesus does not want to be associated with the military and political dynamics of his day within Judaism. Many people had the flawed belief that the Messiah would rescue them from foreign domination.

Milton: The Zealots wanted a Messiah/leader to help them overthrow the Romans. Many thought Jesus could be that person. Judas may have been a closet Zealot who wanted to force Jesus to use his amazing powers in leading the revolt. That is probably why Judas turns Jesus over to Temple officials. The Zealot revolt did occur. It eventually brought about the starvation of the masses and the eventual destruction of Jerusalem in 70 CE by the Roman General Titus.

Anita: Mark's gospel tells us:

> Then he began to teach them that the Son of Man must undergo great suffering, and be rejected by the elders, the chief priests, and the scribes, and be killed, and after three days rise again. He said all this quite openly. And Peter took him aside and began to rebuke him. But turning and looking at his disciples, he rebuked Peter and said, "Get behind me, Satan! For you are setting your mind not on divine things but on human things."[45]

Mary: Does Jesus call Peter Satan because Peter reminds Jesus of his temptations in the wilderness?

Anita: Yes. Jesus refuses to take Satan's way. And Jesus wants to know whether his uncomprehending disciples understand the meaning and effect of his passion and the path they will need to follow. What do you think Jesus means when he says to Peter, "Get away from me, Satan. Your thoughts don't come from God but from man!"

Mary: People do not want to suffer and be rejected by others. They also fear death and do not want to die.

Milton: God's ways are different from people's ways.

Thomas: But if Jesus is the Messiah, he can use his power to achieve whatever he wants. Jesus should not have to suffer to rule.

Anita: Jesus tries to make it clear that before there may be glory and vindication, there will be suffering, death, and resurrection. If Peter and the other disciples want to be part of Jesus' kingdom, they must deny themselves and commit themselves to Jesus and his mission. They are to follow after him, not lead him.

Thomas: Exactly what does that mean?

Anita: Denial of self means we are to stop grasping for everything that will consume our lives and divert us from God's purposes for us in life. Our cross and our lives should be devoted to the carrying on of Jesus' mission in this world. We need to identify ourselves and our actions with Jesus' self-giving love.

Mary: Is that why we pray in the Lord's Prayer *Thy kingdom come. Thy will be done on earth as it is in heaven*?

Anita: Yes. We are praying that God's kingdom will take root in our hearts. God's kingdom is established through faith, love, and forgiveness and not through power wielded by the sword. In the Kingdom of God, we set aside our own plans and are willing to be Jesus' heart, voice, and hands.

Thomas: But what is *God's will*?

Milton: I like to think of it as unity, peace, wholeness, joy, goodness, and righteousness.

Mary: Additionally, it is purity, fidelity, love, hope, faithfulness, and self-giving.

Thomas: Well, it seems as though God's will is often forgotten, disobeyed, or ignored.

Anita: True. People long for God's will to be done here on earth so long as it is on their terms and in alignment with their personal interests.

Milton: That is why Jesus says we have to deny ourselves, take up our cross, and follow him. One of my favorite stories about an early Christian who did just that is the story of Telemachus. We know about him from the writings of Theodoret, Bishop of Cyrrhus in Syria (393-457 CE).

Anita: Tell us about him.

Milton: It is believed Telemachus led a life of pleasure and indulgence before being converted to Christianity. After conversion, he decided to live in seclusion in the desert where he could meditate, fast, and pray. Then it came to him that his love for God was selfish and not selfless, that he needed to go and work in the cities where self-indulgence and sin thrived.

Around 404 CE he traveled over land and sea until he reached Rome, the power center of the world and now a Christian city. Upon his arrival in Rome, he found himself in the midst of a holiday celebrating General Stilicho's victory over the Goths. A triumphal parade with Emperor Honorius alongside Stilicho led to the Coliseum that seated 80,000 people. So Telemachus joined the crowd. After the chariot races ended, men captured in war and then trained as gladiators came out to fight each other to the death. The blood thirsty crowd cheered them on. Telemachus was appalled.

He jumped into the arena wearing his shabby monk's garb and repeatedly cried out to the crowd, "In the name of Jesus, Stop!" For a while, he dodged the stones the enraged crowd threw at him for interrupting their entertaining blood sport. When they began to understand what Telemachus was shouting and that he was not a clown for comic relief, it was too late. Silence fell over the crowd. A sword penetrated Telemachus' body as he lay sprawled on the ground. "In the name of Jesus, Stop!"

A stunned crowd sat in silence for a long time. A holy man had been killed and Christians had participated in the killing. Then one by one everyone left the arena. From that day forward an edict by the emperor ended all gladiatorial games.

Thomas: I wish I could have a faith like Telemachus and could shout to the crowds, "In the name of Jesus, Stop!" Stop the pain brought about by evil, greed, and corruption. Stop the hunger. Stop predatory practices of evil people! Stop the wars! Stop the self-serving ideologies that distort reality and mislead people. Look at what Telemachus accomplished by risking and losing his life. He stopped the gladiatorial games. Wow!

Anita: Thomas, as Jesus would say, you are not far from the Kingdom of God.

With a heavy heart, Jesus leaves the countryside and small villages where he preached, taught, and healed people. He turns his footsteps toward Jerusalem. Before entering Jerusalem, he overlooks the city from the Mount of Olives and weeps. He says:

> If you, even you, had only recognized on this day the things that make for peace! But now they are hidden from your eyes. Indeed, the days will come upon you, when your enemies will set up ramparts around you and surround you, and hem you in on every side. They will crush you to the ground, you and your children within you, and they will not leave within you one stone upon another; because you did not recognize the time of your visitation from God.[46]

Milton: As I already mentioned, Titus destroyed Jerusalem in 70 CE.

Anita: Jesus weeps over Jerusalem because the Jewish people are blindly following false leaders who are leading them to slavery and death. Temple officials, who are living in luxury, are devouring poor people's resources in exchange for a promised spot in heaven.

Jesus' historic entry into Jerusalem is celebrated by the Christian Church on Palm Sunday, often called Passion Sunday. Jesus rides into Jerusalem on a colt. There are at least two symbolic reasons for choosing a colt. What do you think they are?

Milton: Anything used for sacred purposes could not have been ridden upon before. Jesus is making a symbolic, sacred statement about himself. He is fulfilling Zechariah's prophecies regarding the Messiah.

> Lo, your king comes to you triumphant and victorious is he, humble and riding on a donkey, on a colt, the foal of a donkey.[47]

Edward: Yes. A colt is not a horse and therefore signifies that Jesus is not a conquering hero or warrior. He enters Jerusalem humbly and not in glory.

Anita: Jerusalem was a large city of approximately 30,000 to 40,000 year-round residents. During Passover the population swelled to approximately 150,000 people. The crowd that greets Jesus probably includes pilgrims and residents. His entry into Jerusalem is deliberate. He goes directly to the Temple, looks around, and goes to Bethany to spend the night.

The next day he returns to the Temple. He overturns the moneychangers' tables and drives out those who sell animals and birds for sacrifice.

Thomas: Well, this behavior is not one of a meek and mild Jesus. It gives me a different image of Jesus. But why does he act so?

Sarah: Temple officials and most religious people of the time believed it was necessary to exchange money used in everyday life for money used exclusively in the Temple. There were two reasons for this exchange of one kind of money for another. Roman coinage had a picture of Caesar on it. It was a graven image and a violation of the second of the Ten Commandments. And money used and handled in everyday life was considered ritually unclean.

Milton: As a result, the exchange of money may have started as an innocent public service which turned into a full-scale, profitable banking business run by greedy Temple officials. Pilgrims first had to pay a Temple tax equal to two days' wages plus the tax for exchanging the coinage. Also, animals or doves purchased outside the Temple were found to be ritually unclean and were not allowed inside the Temple. Sacrificial animals purchased inside the Temple were considered unblemished and could be priced as much as 75 times higher than those purchased outside the Temple. Pilgrims, many of whom were poor, were swindled and exploited by the commercialization of religion.

Thomas: That means the Temple officials exploit about 150,000 people during their religious holidays. The Temple coffers had to be overflowing.

Anita: Yes. Another sacred violation that angers Jesus is the moneychangers and their stalls that are set up to sell animals and birds in the Court of the Gentiles. Gentiles are barred from worshiping with Jewish people. The noise, commerce, and bedlam in this place make it a shopping bazaar and not a place of worship for Gentiles.

Jesus accuses Temple officials and vendors of turning God's house of prayer into a den of robbers.[48] He believes that the Jewish people are meant to be a beacon light to all the nations of the world. They are not to keep God just to themselves. God loves all people not just the Jews. Jesus wants to wipe away Temple abuses. In Mark 11:17, Jesus says:

> Is it not written, 'My house shall be called a house of prayer for all the nations'?
>
> But you have made it a den of robbers.

Milton: Also, by excluding Gentiles and women from the inner sanctuaries and places of worship, the Temple authorities practice a form of religious discrimination. And the Zealots use the Temple as a safe meeting place and as a hideout to plot their next wave of terrorist activities against the Romans.

Thomas: Many jihadists do the same today within some of their mosques.

Anita: That's true. For less than a week, Jesus teaches openly in the Temple. His message does not change much from the good news he preached in the countryside. But now he is on the home turf of the religious authorities. He warns the people:

> Beware of the scribes, who like to walk around in long robes, and to be greeted with respect in the marketplaces, and to have the best seats in the synagogues and places of honor at banquets! They devour widows' houses and for the sake of appearance say long prayers. They will receive the greater condemnation.[49]

Jesus abhors the abuse of the religious leaders' position and authority.

And he gives the following parable which indicts the religious leaders and Temple officials.

> A man planted a vineyard, put a fence around it, dug a pit for the wine press, and built a watchtower; then he leased it to tenants and went to another country. When the season came, he sent a slave to the tenants to collect from them his share

> of the produce of the vineyard. But they seized him, and beat him, and sent him away empty-handed. And again he sent another slave to them; this one they beat over the head and insulted. Then he sent another, and that one they killed. And so it was with many others; some they beat, and others they killed. He had still one other, a beloved son. Finally he sent him to them, saying, 'They will respect my son.' But those tenants said to one another, 'This is the heir; come, let us kill him, and the inheritance will be ours.' So they seized him, killed him, and threw him out of the vineyard. What then will the owner of the vineyard do? He will come and destroy the tenants and give the vineyard to others. Have you not read this scripture: 'The stone that the builders rejected has become the cornerstone'?[50]

Sarah: Isaiah had a similar parable.[51] He told the people that God had planted Israel as a vineyard owner plants a proper vineyard. God planted the vineyard in good soil and protected it from outside enemies by growing a protective hedge around it and by building a watchtower. The vineyard yielded wild, useless grapes and the vineyard, Israel, was destroyed by the Babylonians.

Jesus' parable reflects Jewish adverse possession laws. If the owner of the land did not make his claim on the land, vineyard workers could go into the Jewish courts and ask that the land be put in their name.

Anita: Jesus uses Isaiah's parable and reformulated it about his and Israel's fate. The religious leaders realize this interpretation of Isaiah's parable is an indictment against them. They want to arrest Jesus but fear the crowd listening to him. Why?

Mary: The people probably agree with Jesus.

Edward: An arrest would create a terrible riot.

Anita: Yes. Tensions between Jesus and Temple officials mount. The verbal picture that Jesus draws represents the following.

- The vineyard represents Israel.
- The vine growers stand for the Jewish rulers and religious leaders.
- The hedge represents the Law which is supposed to instruct and protect the people.
- The winepress represents the fruits of the Law and Jewish peoples' mission for God.
- The tower represents the Divine Householder who watches over, guards, and preserves the vineyard.
- The householder represents God who leaves the tenants to tend to the vineyard.
- The sole purpose of the vineyard is to bring forth good fruit.

Why do the religious leaders want to claim the vineyard for themselves?

Mary: They want power over and control of the people and perhaps their money for their use.

Anita: Whom does the owner of the vineyard send to collect his share of the produce?

Milton: First it is his servants represented by Moses and the prophets. Then God in Jesus represents God's beloved son who is sent to collect the rent. Jesus represents God's last merciful attempt to win over God's chosen people.

Anita: What happens to the son?

Mary: He is seized, killed, and thrown out of the vineyard.

Milton: The irony is that the dead body cannot stay within the vineyard because it will make the vineyard ritually unclean. That is why Jesus foretells his execution will be outside Jerusalem's city walls.

Thomas: Hypocrisy!

Anita: Through this parable Jesus foretells the abusive religious leaders that they will be stripped of their authority which will be given to another. They reach for ownership which is not theirs to have. Jesus becomes the stone that the builders reject and the cornerstone for God's newly chosen people.

Think About It

- Why is Jesus a threat to Herod?
- Should Jesus have gone to Jerusalem?
- Why are Jesus' disciples slow to understand his mission and ultimate suffering? Are we?
- How would you describe God's will?
- How is Telemachus' faith different from the faith of ordinary Christians?
- Would Jesus weep over our country as he did for Jerusalem? What makes you think so?
- Should religious people today take Jesus' warning to beware of the scribes? Why?
- How has the parable of the vineyard changed and how has it remained the same?
- Where should we place ourselves in the parable of the vineyard? Why?

Chapter 10

Jesus Our Suffering Servant

Then the soldiers led him into the courtyard of the palace...and they called together the whole cohort. And they clothed him in a purple cloak; and after twisting some thorns into a crown, they put it on him. And they began saluting him, "Hail, King of the Jews!" They struck his head with a reed, spat upon him, and knelt down in homage to him. After mocking him, they stripped him of the purple cloak and put his own clothes on him. Then they led him out to crucify him.

Mark 15:16-20

Anita: Two days before Passover, the chief priests and scribes decide to look for a way to arrest and kill Jesus. They are afraid to execute their plans during the Passover Festival for fear the crowds will riot. But then Judas makes it possible for them to change their plans. He promises to lead them to Jesus in return for money. We really do not know Judas' motivation. It may have been he was a fanatical nationalist, a Zealot, who wanted to force Jesus to use his amazing power to lead a revolt against Rome.

Milton: Or that he was tired of living the itinerant life of no bed, no board, and no money.

Anita: Could be. Jesus asks Peter and John to prepare for the Passover Meal in Jerusalem. Jesus will not turn back. He knows his disciples well, their weaknesses as well as their strengths. He believes that they will abandon him during his tribulation. He believes death awaits him. Because Jesus knows that this is the last time they will all be together, the Passover meal is very important to him. It commemorates the Jewish people's escape from Egyptian slavery to safety and freedom.

During their supper, Jesus takes off his robe, kneels as a servant would, and washes his disciples' feet. Peter objects. Jesus tells him if he does not let him wash his feet he will not be in fellowship with him. So Peter agrees. Jesus demonstrates what selfless service means. All are on an equal footing. No one is greater and better than someone else.[52]

Mary: That's a great model for ministry.

Anita: Yes. During supper, Jesus says,

> Truly, I say to you, one of you will betray me, one who is eating with me. They began to be distressed and to say to him one after another, "Surely, not I?" He said to them, "It is one of the twelve, one who is dipping bread into the bowl with me. For the Son of Man goes as it is written of him, but woe to that one by whom the Son of Man is betrayed! It would have been better for that one not to have been born."[53]

All the disciples look at Jesus in shock. They grow sorrowful and ask Jesus and one another, "Is it I?"

Jesus does not answer them. Instead he breaks a piece of bread, dips it in the sauce and gives it to Judas Iscariot. As he hands the piece of bread to Judas, Jesus said, "Hurry and do what you must!"

Milton: Perhaps Jesus is offering Judas a second chance and warns him of the eternal consequences if he follows through with his betrayal.

Anita: That's a possibility. But I think Judas is wedded to his plan. He flees from the upper room to the chief priest's room to tell him where they can take Jesus prisoner without a riot occurring. No one but Judas, Jesus, and Temple officials understand the gravity of Judas' plan.

After Judas leaves, Jesus takes a loaf of unleavened bread and after he gives thanks, he breaks it and says, "Take, eat, this is my body which is broken for you. Do this in memory of me." Jesus passes the bread around to his disciples. And when they had all eaten, Jesus takes a cup of wine. He says, "This cup is the new covenant in my blood. Whenever you drink this cup, do so in memory of me." And each disciple drinks from the cup.

Thomas: Wait a minute! I do not understand the significance of the Last Supper. What does it all mean?

Anita: Different Christian denominations interpret the Last Supper differently which eventually became known as the sacrament of the Lord's Supper or Eucharist or Communion. So I won't go into these variations. Instead I will try to give you the meaning of the overall symbolism involved.

- First, you have to be aware that the Last Supper adopts much of the symbolism of the Passover meal and how Jesus relates that symbolism to himself as the Passover Lamb.
- He takes a loaf of bread, blesses it, breaks it and gives it to his disciples. He says the bread is his body which will be broken for all people. It is like the manna the Israelites

gathered in the wilderness to sustain life. This bread is part of God's gift of life. It is often called the bread of heaven.

- Then he takes the cup, blesses it, and passes it around and says it is his blood of the covenant poured out for many. When Jesus speaks about the cup, he thinks of the cup of wrath which is a bitter drink. It is a cup full of painful suffering. Once this cup is emptied by Jesus, it becomes full with his blood and becomes the cup of salvation and the cup of blessing.
- Just as bread is made from many particles of wheat—and wine from many grapes all compressed into the loaf and the cup, so also the breaking and separating of them into small parts at the communion table is symbolic of our sinfulness and brokenness in life which can only be restored to oneness through reconciliation with our neighbors and with God.
- Christians believe they are united with Jesus when they worthily eat the broken bread and drink from the communion cup.

Jesus' death, like the first Passover, liberates people from the legalism of his day and in our time. Through his suffering and death a new covenant between God and believers comes to pass.

The sacrament of the Lord's Supper reminds us of Jesus' sacrificial death and victorious resurrection. Jesus shows us a new way to live and worship. He takes upon himself the consequences of our sins. When believers participate in the Lord's Supper, they inwardly appropriate and participate in Jesus' life, death, and resurrection.

Mary: For me, the Lord's Supper communicates the costly love Jesus paid for us and the price Christians from time to time must pay as well. This costly love is symbolized by the cross, the bread, and the wine.

Thomas: Thank you for this information on the Last Supper.

Anita: After Jesus and his disciples eat, they sing a hymn, leave the upper room, and go toward the Garden of Gethsemane, a private garden that a friend allows him to use. As they walk, Jesus says to them, "You will all fall away from me; for it is written, 'I will strike the shepherd and scatter the sheep.' But after I rise from the dead, I will go before you and meet you in Galilee."

Peter speaks up, "I do not like what you are saying. Master, even though everyone else leaves you, I will never leave you."

And Jesus says to Peter, "Truly, you will fall away from me this very night. Before the cock crows, you will deny me three times."

All of Jesus' disciples vow their loyalty to him. "Nothing," they say, "could frighten us to stay away from you."

When they arrive in the cool of the garden, he tells his disciples to "Sit here while I go off to pray...My heart is overwhelmed with sorrow. My sorrow is so great it almost crushes me. Please pray and watch with me."

Jesus then goes off by himself to pray. Among his other prayers, he prays, "O God! All things are possible for you. Take this cup of suffering away from me. I do not want to die. But I will obey you, come what may."

After praying, Jesus returns to his disciples and finds them asleep. He awakens them and begs, "Can you not stay awake even for one hour? Please, please pray and watch with me."

Then Jesus goes off to pray again. When he returns from praying, he finds his disciples asleep. He awakens them again and cries, "My heart is heavy and sorrowful. Pray and keep watch with me."

When Jesus returns the third time, he tells his disciples, "Wake up. The Son of Man is about to be betrayed and handed over to the power of evil men. Get up, let us be going. See my betrayer is at hand."

Thomas: Oh! I feel his sorrow and sense of thoughtless disregard of his wishes. Why weren't Jesus' disciples alert to the dangers facing him? They should have protected him.

Anita: It's too late. Judas leads

> ...a crowd with swords and clubs, from the chief priests, the scribes, and the elders. Now the betrayer had given them a sign, saying, "The one I will kiss is the man; arrest him and lead him away under guard." So when he came, he went up to him at once and said, "Rabbi!" and kissed him. Then they laid hands on him and arrested him. But one of those who stood near drew his sword and struck the slave of the high priest, cutting off his ear. Then Jesus said to them, "Have you come out with swords and clubs to arrest me as though I were a bandit? Day after day I was with you in the temple teaching, and you did not arrest me. But let the scriptures be fulfilled." All of them deserted him and fled.[54]

Why do you suppose everyone abandons him?

Thomas: Self-preservation. They fear for their lives especially since Jesus offers no resistance.

Milton: Perhaps his disciples lost their opportunity to protect him for not being on watch. But there is an unidentified person who could have been Peter who strikes a blow for Jesus by cutting off the ear of the high priest's servant. Peter also mingles with the crowd and follows Jesus into the courtyard of the high priest.

Anita: The arresting mob arrives under orders given by the Sanhedrin, the court in Jerusalem that governs Jewish religious and political life during and before the Christian era. The Sanhedrin is under Roman domination and consists of 71 members presided over by a High Priest who cooperates with Roman authorities. The Sanhedrin does not have the authority to execute a death penalty. That right belongs to the Roman Governor and has to be carried out by Roman authorities.

Milton: That is true. But the Sanhedrin flagrantly violates all their laws by which they govern.

Thomas: How so?

Milton: Let's look at the mockery of Jesus' trial. We do not know whether they had the necessary quorum of 23. The Sanhedrin is not allowed to meet at night nor during the great feasts such as Passover. Both conditions they violated. Court was to be held within the Temple precincts. It was not. The passage of one night must occur before the execution of the death penalty. It never happens. Members of the Sanhedrin are unable to get two witnesses' stories to agree. Then the high priest does the forbidden and unthinkable by asking a leading question. It was against their law to force a person to incriminate himself.

Thomas: What was the question?

Milton: "Are you the Messiah, the Son of the Blessed One?" Jesus answers, "I am; and 'you will see the Son of Man seated at the right hand of the Power,' and 'coming with the clouds of heaven.'"[55]

Sarah: "Blessed One" is the Jewish way of referring to God. Personally, I was unaware of the Sanhedrin's violation of their rules when it came to Jesus' trial. Even so, a handful of misguided and corrupt Jewish leaders should not or could not have created the anti-Semitism that grew out of their deadly behavior.

Anita: I agree. Other than for Pilate and his Roman Army, everyone involved in Jesus crucifixion and death is a Jew. The Sanhedrin finds Jesus guilty of blasphemy. That means they believe he speaks disrespectfully about God and his relationship to God. There upon, the high priest tears his clothes and asks for the death penalty. His contrived outrage succeeds in his getting the Sanhedrin to vote for Jesus' death.

The Sanhedrin members present demonstrate their frenzied hatred and antipathy toward Jesus in their unseemly behavior towards him.

Thomas: Such as?

Anita: "Some began to spit on him, to blindfold him, and to strike him, saying to him, 'Prophesy!' The guards also beat him."[56]

Thomas: I am glad that I am free to express my doubts and thoughts without judicial or religious condemnation.

Mary: I can understand why Peter denies knowing Jesus. At that time, he did not fully comprehend who Jesus is or what it means to be the Messiah. He does not believe suffering to be part of God's divine plan.

Anita: True. Only Peter was brave enough to mingle in the courtyard of the high priest while Jesus stands trial. When he is recognized as a follower of Jesus by a servant girl of the high priest, he denies knowing Jesus three different times before the cock crows as forecasted by Jesus.

Milton: I think the take away from this account is that we are to do better than Peter.

Anita: Yes. In the morning, members of the Sanhedrin turn Jesus over to Pilate. They accuse Jesus of sedition and treason because he calls himself the King of the Jews. Pilate suspects the motives of the Temple authorities. He thinks they are jealous of Jesus. Pilate tries to release Jesus by means of his Passover custom of releasing a prisoner. He takes a murderer and insurrectionist, Barabbas, and Jesus onto his balcony and asks the crowd to decide whom he should release.

Milton: Big mistake. He should have anticipated the chief priests' manipulation of the mob. Pilate is cornered. He wants to please the crowd. And he fears reprisals from Rome if he does not keep the peace and if he allows a pretender to the throne to remain alive.

Anita: After Pilate orders his soldiers to take Jesus away, they unmercifully torture him. Here is a brief summary of what happened.

"Hail to the King of the Jews!" a soldier exclaims in mocking disbelief.

The soldiers find a purple cloak which they drape around Jesus. They get some thorny branches and twist them together to make a crude crown. They push it down on Jesus' head. Stepping back, the soldiers look at their handiwork and grin mean grins.

They spit on Jesus, and they insult him. But Jesus stands calmly and quietly. He never reacts or even moves. He is resigned to his fate and wordlessly and calmly tolerates their cruelty.

Jesus' demeanor frightens the soldiers. Why does this man stand so motionlessly, his face expressionless? Their efforts to humiliate him fail. Jesus stands before them with dignity.

Milton: Also, they scourge him with his hands tied to a post. The whip they use is made with knotted cord or leather straps often weighted with pieces of metal or bone to tear his skin and increase his torture.

Anita: The crown of thorns bites deeply into Jesus' scalp causing blood to trickle down his forehead into his eyes.

The soldiers notice the calmness with which Jesus endures his pain. They feel guilty at mistreating this man who shows such courage. They also feel afraid. Their fear in turn makes them angry at themselves. So they forcefully order Jesus to pick up the cross beam to his cross and enter onto the streets of Jerusalem.

Milton: Did you know that crucifixion was a mode of execution originated in Persia and adopted by the Greeks and Romans as a form of punishment reserved for lower-class criminals, foreigners, and slaves.

The Roman cross consisted of two beams. On his way to Golgotha, Jesus carries the cross beam, not the entire cross. The entire cross would be too heavy for most men to carry.

Anita: Yes. Also, Jesus' physical condition has deteriorated. He did not sleep the night before, nor had he eaten or had anything to drink since his last supper with his disciples. His cross grows heavier and heavier. Weak from hunger, scourging, and loss of blood, Jesus walks more and more slowly, stumbling with every step until he falls, unable to get up and go any farther.

The crowd taunts him. "Get up! Get up! Where is your God now? If you really are the Messiah, if you really are the Son of God, get up and save yourself! Summon some angels—have them save you!"

Jesus ignores the crowd. He tries to stand up, but he can't lift the cross. He almost makes it, but then collapses once again beneath the weight of the cross. Annoyed with the delay, a soldier drags someone out of the crowd.

"You! What's your name?" the impatient officer demands.

"Simon. But I'm from Cyrene—I'm not involved with this," the nervous man sputters.

"I don't care where you're from or what you're doing here. You're going to carry this man's cross."

Seeking frantically for an excuse which would get him out of this situation, Simon looks at the soldier. He wants to protest. He wants to say no. But then Simon looks at Jesus crumpled underneath the heavy cross, still struggling to get up. Simon goes over and picks up the cross. When he does so, Jesus looks up and gives Simon a look of thanks. Simon then quickly shoulders the cross and moves on. He is in awe of the pained majesty of the man whose cross he now carries.

At last they reach Golgotha where the execution takes place. Jesus is stripped and nailed to the cross beam of the cross. Slowly the soldiers raise him up on the vertical beam of the cross. On this vertical portion of the cross, there is a projecting peg for his feet which carry some of his weight so as to prevent his nailed hands from tearing away from the cross.

Milton: Golgotha is the name of the place where Jesus is crucified. Its Greek name is Calvary. It is located outside the city walls and is on a hill visible from the city. It is a place where executions take place. Skulls may be scattered on the ground. Also, the place was skull shaped.

Death by crucifixion is protracted. Dehydration, loss of blood, hunger, oxygen deprivation, and exhaustion are the direct cause of death. The only relief permitted a victim is a stupefying draught or drink. It sometimes takes three or four days for death to occur.

Anita: Once again the crowd taunts Jesus. They shout at him to save himself. Even one of the thieves crucified with Jesus joins in.

So you're the King of the Jews. Pleased to make your acquaintance, your Majesty. I'm glad I'm dying in such distinguished company. I mean us common folk aren't usually given such honors. But, King Jesus, why don't you make a royal gesture? Something magnificent! Something spectacular! I know—save yourself. And while you are at it—save us!"

But the other thief isn't so mean-spirited. "Why don't you shut up? Haven't you got any fear of God? Haven't you heard Jesus speak? Yeah, we're all being crucified together, but we deserve it. He doesn't. We're thieves. We've committed crimes. But Jesus, he hasn't done anything wrong!" the thief declares passionately.

Then in quiet tones the thief speaks to Jesus, "Lord, I heard you speak. You were real good. I wanted to repent and lead a good life, but as you can see it was a little late when I finally heard you. I don't know, Lord. I haven't really got any right to ask anything of you. But Lord, will you please remember me when you come as King?"

Jesus smiles weakly, "It isn't too late. I tell you, and I tell you truly, you will be with me in Paradise before the night is out."

Jesus gasps. Death approaches. He feels all alone. Where are his disciples? Why have they abandoned him? Not once have they come looking for him. The only disciple he saw was John whom he charged to look after his mother. Jesus never saw another disciple's familiar face appear in the crowd to give him a smile of love and silent support. And God? Had God left him just like his disciples? In anguish, Jesus cried out, "My God! My God! Why have you forsaken me?"

The sky blackens for three hours. Then Jesus utters, "It is finished. Father, into your hands I commend my spirit."[57]

And, with this last agonizing whisper, Jesus breaths his last breath.

The earth quakes. Rocks shatters. The curtain in the Temple tears in two. An officer who had earlier recognized Jesus' quiet dignity draws back in fear. Then fear turns to awe. "That man—He really was the Son of God!"

These events surrounding Jesus' death and the days to come tell us that God will not let Jesus' death be the end. Jesus will rise from the dead, and evil will never again be able to harm him or control him.

Think About It

- Pretend you are one of Jesus' disciples. How would you have behaved toward Jesus during Holy Week?
- Why is Jesus called the Passover Lamb?
- What are your thoughts on the Last Supper?
- What thoughts do you have on Judas' betrayal? On Peter's denial? On Jesus' disciples' flight and abandonment of him?
- Historically, Jews have been accused of deicide—that they killed God. Should they be held responsible for Jesus' death? What makes you think so?

Chapter 11

Reflections on Jesus' Final Words on the Cross, Part I

Father, forgive them; for they do not know what they are doing.

Luke 23:24

Anita: We know that all but one of Jesus' disciples forsook him. Only John and the women had the courage to be with him on Golgotha.

Jesus is not a helpless victim. He allows himself to be mocked by the soldiers and made to wear a crown of thorns pressed into his scalp causing his blood to run down his face and into his eyes. His skin is ripped open and bleeds from scourging.

Milton: Yet he refuses to respond to his mockers' taunts and do as they wish. Perhaps he connects their taunts and challenges with those he experienced with Satan in the wilderness. Those who mock him say, "He saved others; he cannot save himself. Let the Messiah, the King of Israel, come down from the cross now, so that we may see and believe."[58]

Anita: Today, I want us to take a closer look at Jesus' first words from the cross, what he says, and what lessons we can learn from them. There are several different approaches we can take regarding the crucifixion. If we were to ask what happened, we would look for clues in order to file a report similar to a police report. If we were to ask what Jesus' last words and crucifixion mean to us as believers, we are asking questions of faith. Let's pursue this latter approach.

The gospel accounts of Jesus' passion are quite lengthy compared to the rest of the individual gospels. Yet when we read them, we get very few details on his crucifixion. The people of Jesus' time knew the horrors of crucifixion and needed no graphic illustrations. Rome lined its roads and even entire villages with crucified civilians, insurrectionists, and zealots.

That is why I think the gospel writers concentrated on the tenor and mood of the crowd and Jesus.

Thomas: It could be his persecutors wanted to see Jesus fight back. It took courage for him not to give in to that temptation.

Anita: What would you have done?

Thomas: Me? I would have fought back. In the first place, I would never have gone to Jerusalem and put myself in harm's way. Nor would I let myself be captured in the Garden of Gethsemane. I would have then escaped the farce of a trial before the Sanhedrin. And if I were their prisoner, I would never have responded to the high priest's question that incriminated me. I would have defended myself before Pilate. Any survivor would have done the same.

Anita: I think most of us would have done likewise. Jesus' crucifixion is a time of darkness and evil. His crucifixion does not occur behind closed doors. It is out in the open for all to witness.

Mary: Additionally, hatred is masked in self-righteousness. The cross shows us the twisted work of the powers of darkness. Jesus' cross symbolizes evil's attack on the innocent.

Thomas: I think the religious authorities want to make Jesus a non-person with no past and no future. How dare he challenge them and their rule? Jesus' crucifixion is an example of sanctioned violence by political and religious authorities that want to hold onto power. People in authority crucify dissidents and their enemies spiritually, psychologically, emotionally, politically, and/or physically. Look at all the evil committed supposedly in God's name by religious cults and radical Islam such as Boko Haram, ISIS, Al Qaeda. They use fear and intimidation to control and manipulate people.

Sarah: I agree with you Thomas.

Anita: Remember those who received their miraculous cures from Jesus? They do not stand up to help Jesus. On the long route to Golgotha, a Roman officer carried a placard before Jesus that identified the charges against him. Legally, if someone could refute the charges against Jesus, the procession would be stopped and his case retried. No one came to his defense.

Thomas: It figures. They were afraid of the consequences if they challenged the authorities. They probably returned to the comfort of their homes. Perhaps what was important to them was their cure—not Jesus.

Anita: Let us try to understand Jesus' thoughts by examining his Seven Last Words on the cross. While thinking about what he says, keep in mind his physical pain and his psychological distress and feelings of abandonment.

The first words that come from him are, "Father, forgive them; for they do not know what they are doing."[59]

What do you think of his appeal to God to forgive those who crucify him?

Thomas: If we are honest with ourselves, we know we all sin every time we harm an innocent person, inflict pain, show contempt, and mock someone. We, like them, want forgiveness. But that is not happening among the mob. They do not seek forgiveness.

Mary: For me, Jesus' words assure me that we, who seek forgiveness and repent of our sins, are forgiven when we promise God and ourselves that we will turn from sin and darkness to receive God's loving grace.

Milton: Yes. And that we, in turn, should forgive those who sin against us. As we say in the Lord's Prayer, "And forgive us our trespasses as we forgive those who trespass against us." To confess our sins or trespasses is to take responsibility for them. True confession is a sign of faith maturity.

Thomas: I know we talked about repentance in an earlier discussion. But tell me again what repentance is?

Anita: Repentance is turning away from sin and evil. It is a conversion and orientation to God. True repentance leads to a clean heart and a change in attitude and deeds.

Forgiveness for sins committed is conditional on the perpetrator

- naming the sin committed,
- accepting the blame for it,
- sincere repentance and remorse,
- and, if possible, restitution.

Forgiveness also requires the victim to let go of hate and all thoughts of retribution and revenge. By the way, hate in biblical terminology means to love less. It does not mean to despise someone.

Forgiveness does not mean the offense did not matter. It did. But we must not be held captive by the perpetrator and the offense even if the perpetrator does not seek forgiveness. Like a dead leaf, we must let it fall from our hearts and leave our thoughts. Then we need to let go of it and let it float down a fast moving stream to its destiny. God is our judge who passes judgment—not us.

Sarah: Let me challenge you on your beliefs on forgiveness. As you know, a large number of my family was killed in Nazi Germany during the Holocaust. In Simon Wiesenthal's *The Sunflower,* he questions whether he should forgive a wounded and dying 21-year old Nazi SS soldier, Karl, who participated in atrocities towards the Jews. Hitler's SS soldiers were dedicated to surveillance and terror within Germany and conquered countries. They also were responsible for the extermination of Jews and dissidents. One such horror occurred when Karl and his platoon were ordered to round up all the Jews in the Russian village of Dnepropetrovsk. They crammed about 400 men, women, and children into a house which they torched. They shot anyone who tried to escape the incineration. Karl and the other soldiers did as they were commanded.

As Karl lay dying, he asks a Red Cross nurse in the concentration camp to find and send a Jew to him. She picks Simon who hears Karl's confession. He seeks Simon's absolution for his crimes. Karl says:

> "I want to die in peace, and so I need..."
>
> I saw that he (Karl) could not get the words past his lips. But I was in no mood to help him. I kept silent.
>
> "I know that what I have told you is terrible. In the long nights while I have been waiting for death, time and time

> again I have longed to talk about it to a Jew and beg forgiveness from him. Only I didn't know whether there were any Jews left….
>
> "I know that what I am asking is almost too much for you, but without your answer I cannot die in peace."[60]

All of Simon's family had been exterminated. He did not know how many days of life were left for him before his extermination. He did not say a word to Karl. He stood up and left the death chamber. Yet all the time he was with Karl he held his hand, gave him a drink of water, and brushed away the flies swarming over him.

In 1946, four years after Karl's death, Simon visited Karl's mother and listened to her eulogy of her son's goodness. Simon left without exposing Karl's evil deeds to his mother.

Even today, children, like the youthful Karl, are indoctrinated with "Fuhrers" who have replaced God that lead people to hate and violence.

Simon Wiesenthal puts these questions to all of us.

- What would you have done in his place?
- Who are we to forgive a murderer whose victims are no longer alive?
- As a third party, can you speak and forgive on behalf of the victims or can only the victims make that decision?

Edward: I am not sure what I would do even if I were a Jew. Who am I to forgive individuals, a tribe, or country for the genocide carried out against them? I am not the victim. I lack the power to grant forgiveness. I think Simon showed mercy and compassion by not telling Karl's mother of her son's evil acts against the Jews. I think she really knew of his and Germany's crimes against humanity. She probably lived in denial in order to survive the fear and intimidation brought on by Hitler and his men.

Mary: But as a Christian we are supposed to forgive if we want forgiveness for ourselves.

Thomas: Are you thinking like Karl in terms of beliefs that may not fit the crime? Karl seemed more concerned about his own soul than the souls he murdered. Why did he wait to repent on his deathbed and not before? Simon did not know what was in Karl's heart. He didn't seem to care or know whether any Jews were still alive so long as he had a Jew at his bedside to absolve him of his crimes. He could have called for a priest instead of a Jew.

Sarah: We Jews believe that the only path toward forgiveness is to be free of anger and hatred. We must first seek forgiveness from the person we wronged. And as Elie Wiesel has said, "How can I forgive, really, for everybody? Who authorized me to be the representative of six million men, women, children and say in their name I forgive? Never!"

Anita: Thank you Sarah. You challenge our Christian beliefs and hopefully cause us to think more deeply about forgiveness. I think Jesus' compassion and mercy towards his persecutors are similar to Simon's. Jesus' appeal to God indicates to me that God is the final judge on forgiveness. Jesus' persecutors, like Karl, were blindly following orders that perpetuate evil originating from and operating through earthly authorities.

Sarah: The Jewish people then, and now, have a penitential season known as the Ten Days of Penitence that begin on Rosh Hashanah and culminate on Yom Kippur, our Day of Atonement. During this time, we Jews examine our souls for the past year, ask forgiveness of those we have wronged, and make restitution for the sins we have committed. Only when we ask for forgiveness from those we harm, do we believe we can come before God and hope for forgiveness.

Mary: In one of our meetings, we talked about the parable of the lost sheep and the Prodigal Son. But these parables weren't about horrific evils such as Jesus' crucifixion or the Holocaust.

Thomas: How important is it for God's people to forgive perpetrators who commit atrocities that kill or maim their victims? Can we forgive terrorists' attacks in Boston, Paris, Mali, San Bernardino, and other locations? Has this country forgiven Osama bin Laden and his Al Qaeda terrorists for the World Trade Center attack that killed over 2977 people and deprived their families of them? What about the killing fields of Cambodia, the murder of Armenians by the Turks, the murder of Ukrainians and other ethnic groups by Stalin, the Jewish/Palestinian murders, the Hutus' massacre of the Tutsi, Saddam Hussein's use of biological weapons against the Kurdish people, the capture and sale of women by jihadists, American genocide of native Americans and theft of their property, the black slave trade and slavery, KKK, and all other hate dynasties? Can we or should we forgive perpetrators of their crimes against humanity? These evil doers have not sought forgiveness nor are they repentant. We delude ourselves when we say we forgive those people who are unrepentant, brutish, and incorrigible? But have we actually forgiven them? Must these evil doers be forgiven by me and others? I think not.

Anita: Clergy are often called upon by parishioners to explain to them the limits of forgiveness. Christian forgiveness is a complex, difficult subject which is often misunderstood and misinterpreted. Jesus had a lot to say about forgiveness. He was a first century Jew who used the Jewish moral framework for life, sin, repentance, and forgiveness.

Let me address your response to massive crimes to a local crime in Betty Jane Spencer's Indiana farmhouse. A group of young men high on drugs broke into her farmhouse. They killed her sons and left her for dead. All men were convicted of their crime and sent to prison. While in prison, one murderer claimed he found Christ. He wrote Betty Jane and asked her to forgive him. She went to her pastor and asked him if she were obligated as a Christian to forgive this man. Her pastor, Richard P. Lord, asked her to give him six months to answer her question. He spoke to other victims of violence and found that most victims could not forgive perpetrators who victimized them or a loved one. One mother mournfully concluded that she would rather go to hell for her lack of forgiveness even though the murderer could possibly go to heaven.

Then Richard Lord asks, "Does finding Christ excuse what was done? Does a religious experience mean that now Christians should act as though a crime wasn't committed?" Were the prison ministers off in left field when they recommended that Betty Jane Spencer forgive one of the murderers of her sons who also left her for dead? Just because he became a Christian, he thinks he must be forgiven by her so that he can be released from prison to witness for Christ? Betty Jane wondered, "Why can't he witness in prison?"

Edward: It seems the Christian church places a double burden upon Christian victims. Must these victims endure the initial violation as well as the Christian duty to forgive?

Anita: Richard Lord told Betty Jane she did not have to establish a relationship with her sons' murderer, that she did not have to be responsible for his salvation, and that she did not have to forgive him. Her sons' murderer was seeking *cheap grace* from her.

Thomas: I agree. Tell us again what is cheap grace?[61]

Anita: German theologian Dietrich Bonhoeffer coined this terminology. He was hanged as a Nazi resistor in 1945. In his book *The Cost of Discipleship,* Bonhoeffer describes cheap grace as grace sold in the marketplace like shoddy, inferior goods. He probably had in mind the Dominican friar Johann Tetzel's jingle for increasing the sale of indulgences. "As soon as the coin in the coffer rings, the soul from purgatory springs."

Thomas: What then are indulgences?

Mary: Catholics believe Jesus' sacrifice left an infinite treasury of merits in the Church for the benefit of sinners. In Medieval times, people believed a person could purchase from a Vatican salesman an indulgence from this treasury. The benefit received from such a purchase would be less time and physical torment that a person must endure in Purgatory. We believe the purchased indulgence for a particular person dead or alive helps remove the sins of a particular person.

Anita: Martin Luther challenged the sale of indulgences which precipitated the Protestant Reformation. His Thesis 32 says, "All those who believe themselves certain of their own salvation by means of letters of indulgence, will be eternally damned, together with their teachers." And Thesis 37 says, "Any true Christian whatsoever, living or dead, participates in all the benefits of Christ and the Church, and this participation is granted to him by God without letters of indulgence."[62]

Thomas: In other words, indulgences purchased as a means to salvation and eternal life is useless.

Anita: Yes. Bonhoeffer believed that grace should change you and make you a disciple of Jesus Christ. If a person's inner life remains unchanged, all formula, ritual or indulgences are useless. Bonhoeffer writes:

> Costly grace confronts us as a gracious call to follow Jesus; it comes as a word of forgiveness to the broken spirit and the contrite heart. Grace is costly because it compels a man to submit to the yoke of Christ and follow him; it is grace because Jesus says: "My yoke is easy and my burden is light."[63]

Thomas: Well, then, you could say that Betty Jane's murderer falls into the category of costly grace?

Anita: Yes and no. We do not know what was in his heart. Was he using his supposed conversion as an escape route out of prison? I have to agree with Betty Jane that costly grace should cause him to want to minister to other prisoners and not to seek his personal freedom. Then he could work out his penance in prison.

Milton: Today, too many Christians have accepted a sound-bite approach to sin and forgiveness. They overlook the nuances and the Jewish religious/cultural time period and framework when Jesus expressed his thoughts and the complicated circumstances surrounding repentance, forgiveness, and reconciliation.

Anita: Correct. We should not look upon forgiveness as a commercial transaction. If we ask for forgiveness and are given it, we in turn should not withhold it from others who genuinely seek our forgiveness. That is why we ask God to forgive our trespasses as we forgive those who trespass against us. We are not the judge and jury. God is.

We also ask God to "Lead us not into temptation, but deliver us from evil." At first glance, the first part of this petition could be mistaken to mean that God leads us into temptation. That is not what Jesus had in mind when he gave us this petition. This petition does mean, however, that temptation and testing are a part of our daily lives. Faith in God does not guarantee the good life and freedom from harm. Our temptations and testing help prepare us for the ultimate temptation in life. Jesus talks about deliverance from major evil over which we do not have sufficient resources ourselves to defeat. Jesus alerts us to the forces of evil that can cause us to forsake our faith and the doing of God's will.

In the second part of this petition, we pray for God's help and deliverance. "Jesus' cross, death, and resurrection tell us that evil can destroy us physically and weaken us spiritually, that God is with us and suffers with us, but eventually God has the last word."[64] A major part of forgiveness is a letting go.

Edward: I wonder about 21-year old Dylann Roof, a white supremacist. On June 17, 2015, he joined a bible study group at Emanuel African Methodist Episcopal Church in Charleston, S.C. He was silent for about an hour. Then he shot nine attendees. He allowed five to survive to tell the world what he had done. He hoped to start a race war. Instead, in court, many victims' family members forgave Dylann. Subsequently whites and blacks joined hands and voted for the removal of the Confederate flag from state buildings. Their forgiveness of Dylann is remarkable.

Anita: Indeed. Since there is a certain degree of detachment from the events we have discussed today, I want you to think about those people who may have harmed you physically, emotionally, spiritually, financially, professionally, and/or psychologically. Were you able to forgive them? Why or why not? Were there any consequences?

Then write your thoughts on forgiveness as they relate to Jesus' words from his cross, Simon Wiesenthal's and Betty Jane

Spencer's positions, the Charleston racist killings, and your personal experiences. Put into writing your thoughts for our next meeting. You may wish to keep your specific personal injury done to you to yourself. If so, tell only how you dealt with forgiveness.

Think About It

- What new thoughts about forgiveness did you learn today?
- How do your friends and family deal with forgiveness?
- How can you help them in understanding forgiveness?
- How would forgiveness stop wars and bring peace?

Chapter 12

Can You Forgive?

Forgiving the unrepentant is like drawing pictures on water.

Japanese Proverb

Forgiveness is a letting go. It is the key that unlocks the door and the handcuffs of hate. It is a power that breaks the chains of bitterness and the shackles of selfishness.

Our Lord is in the cleansing business, not the whitewashing business.

Anita: At the conclusion of our last meeting, I asked you to think about Jesus' words on forgiveness from the cross and as they relate to Simon Wiesenthal, Betty Jane Spencer, the Charleston, SC, murders, and your personal experiences. Each of you prepared a statement of your views. I want each one of you to read yours. If we so choose, we can discuss your thoughts after we hear each other's statements. Let's begin.

Edward's Thoughts: As you know, I come from a liberal Protestant background and reject authoritarian religions that claim to represent God's word and law. With that in mind, let me answer the question on forgiveness. I can forgive those people who are forced to carry out state orders such as military personnel but not the ones who issue diabolical orders. Karl represents today's young, radicalized Muslims. He knew what the purposes of the SS were. Yet he willingly joined them as do today's radicalized Muslims join ISIS, Al Qaeda, and other terrorist organizations. Many of these Muslims become disillusioned and find themselves trapped in an endless cycle of violence and evil from which there is no escape. Those who manage to get out may seek forgiveness and rehabilitation. But most don't. Is it because they fear retribution?

Individuals and groups filled with radical evil despise the humanity and worth of people who are different from them.

I don't believe in cheap grace. Therefore, I agree with Reverend Lord's advice to Betty Jane Spencer. Excessive drug and alcohol use is no excuse for the taking of life. The murderers are responsible for their impaired mental state.

I think survivors and relatives of victims of the massacre in Charleston, S.C., may have rushed the many stages of grief and forgiveness toward Dylann Roof. Sometimes I wonder if they meant it completely. He did not seek their forgiveness. Yet, like them, I would not want to be held hostage by evil. I can understand where they are coming from. African Americans would never have survived slavery, intimidation, murder, and all kinds of other injustices if they kept rage, anger, revenge, and hatred in their hearts toward their oppressors. Unfortunately, in the United States and after the Civil War, Abraham Lincoln was assassinated and no one else had the vision much less the courage or compassion to lead a Truth and Reconciliation Commission similar to the one led by Desmond Tutu and Nelson Mandela in South Africa that ended the cycle of violence under apartheid. Consequently, evil has not been named and acknowledged.

It has been perpetuated by hate dynasties. I agree with Bishop Desmond Tutu and what he writes in his book *No Future Without Forgiveness.*

One person in particular has enriched himself at my expense. I do not seek revenge nor reconciliation with him. He has not confessed the harm he has caused me. Nor has he made any attempt at restitution. Forgiveness for me is a sending away or letting go of his offense against me. I believe in divine justice and turn the entire affair over to God.

Milton's Thoughts: My evangelical background and training as a philosopher are in tension with each other and shape much of my thinking, doubt, questioning, and response to evil. I can't even imagine experiencing the horrors of the Holocaust. Simon was one helpless victim among millions. Simon's only remaining possession was his soul. And as a predator, Karl wanted Simon's soul to show God that his victims forgave him. On behalf of the living and the dead, I don't think it was Simon's duty to forgive Karl. In this matter, forgiveness is God's business, not Simon's.

Betty Jane Spencer and her minister weighed genuine forgiveness that comes from the heart versus false forgiveness. I respect their carefully considered decision and probably would have done likewise.

As for the Charleston, S.C. killings, I have to admire victim's families' public forgiveness towards the murderer of their loved ones. Privately, they may be withholding their forgiveness. They probably realized without their public forgiveness they would recycle vengeance, anger, hatred, violence, and cruelty which could lead to personal torment and even race riots. This recycling of revenge would not heal their open wounds or bring back their loved ones. Jesus' cross shows them and us the costliness of forgiveness. As in the past, African Americans have suffered at the hands of slave owners and white supremacists. Most African Americans do not retaliate. In imitation of Jesus, they absorbed Dylann Roof's blows. They and other minorities are God's suffering servants. Jesus shows us that after the evil that caused his crucifixion, there is always a new day brought about by his and our resurrection.

In addition to physical evil, there is psychological, emotional, and spiritual evil. As for the evil done against me, I find it difficult to forgive a person who continuously seeks to undermine my livelihood and credibility. He has never sought my forgiveness and continues to harm me which affects not only me but my family as well. For me to forgive an unrepentant man who has no intention to stop his evil doings towards me is immoral. I will not let myself be victimized by him. I have turned the entire matter over to God. I dismiss this enemy from my thoughts and my presence and do not seek revenge. Nor do I grant him any false forgiveness and false reconciliation. He is a toxic, evil person, and I will not play his game.

Mary's Thoughts: As you know I am struggling with my loss of trust in the Roman Catholic Church's priests. Am I required to forgive my priest who stole parish money to support his partner in a New York City apartment and to pay for his yacht? What about my confessions to him and the absolutions given me through him? Were they meaningless? What about the pedophile priests within the Church and the trauma of their victims? How can their innocence be restored? We were not created to be abused especially by those we should trust. My heart breaks for the victims of their evil and hypocrisy. The effect of unworthy priests and their public exposure on our young people has been devastating.

I think many Roman Catholics have left the church because of this spiritual corruption and its clergy's lack of repentance. Why?

Is it that many priests have chosen not to carry their cross and follow Jesus? Instead they use their position to satisfy their sexual needs and greed. To my knowledge these priests have not publicly repented and sought forgiveness and repentance from those people they harmed. Were they not required to confess their sins at least once a year to their confessor? And no action was taken by their confessor whom I assume was a superior to them? Because they failed to live up to the higher standard required of clergy, for me, they are no longer my role model. Yet I still love my church and have hope that Pope Francis will remove evildoers from it and cleanse the church. I see him as the pilot of a large ship trying to turn the ship around in the narrow waters of the Tiber River. Many of his crew members are out to sabotage him and his reforms.

In the case of Simon Wiesenthal, I would have walked out of Karl's room. I could not forgive a person who waited for approaching death to ask for forgiveness from a Jew. We do not know whether Karl had confessed his sins to a priest. Even in death, Karl was only thinking of himself. And since I am not the offended party, Karl must throw himself on God's mercy.

I agree with Betty Jane Spencer's response to the killer's request for forgiveness. Let the killer work out his repentance within the walls of the jail. Yet she should not let her life and person be defined by this one horrific experience. She needs to let go, heal, and rebuild her life. To do that, I think she needs to turn the act of forgiving over to God. If she so chooses, there is no need for reconciliation with the murderer. But she needs to release herself from the burden of forgiving the murderer.

As for the Charleston murders, I would have taken my time before making a decision. Genuine forgiveness and grieving is a process that comes slowly. And Dylann did not seek their forgiveness.

I have been fortunate not to have any horrific crimes done against me. I can, and do forgive, and let go of all insults, slights, and intentional sins against me.

You have caused me to rethink my beliefs on forgiveness. I am upset by my new thoughts. I will no longer look upon my religion as formulaic. At the same time, I will not forget all the good the Roman Catholic Church has and still does throughout the world with its missions, hospitals, universities, and charities.

Sarah's Thoughts: If Hitler and his industrialized genocide against Jews and other non-Arian groups and resistors had not been so effective, I would have living cousins today. My grandparents, aunts, uncles, and cousins all died in Auschwitz and Sobibor. As you know, my father was a professor at Harvard. So my immediate family was safe in the U.S.

Some of my relatives sold everything they had and paid a small fortune to leave Germany on the ship *MS St. Louis* in 1939. Their destination was Cuba. When they arrived there, an embargo was instituted. They were not allowed to disembark. The United States also refused to accept them. Jews are not terrorists. Yet they have always been a persecuted minority. They sought sanctuary away from Hitler's Germany. Captain Gustav Schroder, a non-Jewish German, considered sinking his ship so coast guards would rescue his passengers and bring them ashore. Instead and in desperation, he returned to Europe and negotiated with the UK, France, Belgium, and the Netherlands to take in his passengers. Of the 936 Jewish passengers, 709 survived the war. My relatives were among the 227 who were exterminated. Captain Schroder was posthumously recognized as one of the Righteous at the Yad Vashem Holocaust Memorial in Israel.

Forgiveness is very personal and utterly relational. Simon had no personal relationship with Karl who in turn probably had none with God. I am in agreement with the victim Simon, who felt pity and compassion for Karl. But it is not within his or my power to play God and forgive Karl and his SS soldiers' crimes.

It is absolutely necessary for Betty Jane and the relatives of the Charleston church victims to let go and pray for God's help to do so. They can show mercy towards the perpetrator who may be mentally unstable and who needs to remain imprisoned for the protection of society. If the victims don't let go, they will remain their perpetrator's victim and will never be able to heal spiritually, emotionally, and mentally from the trauma inflicted upon them. The past cannot be undone. And unless a person is truly remorseful and repentant, I have no desire to grant my forgiveness let alone reconciliation. It is up to God to read a person's heart and soul. It is God who decides whether to forgive. It is God who relieves me of that burden, sorrow, grief, hate, forgiveness, and reconciliation.

After the Paris attacks and the untimely death of loved ones, I will not let some religiously crazed terrorists poison my thoughts and heart. I will not compound their evil or be complicit in it. Instead, I will live on and will try to make this world a better place. I hope evil doers will learn who God really is, repent, and seek God's mercy and forgiveness.

Thomas' Thoughts: Sin and evil stalk this beautiful world. It always has and unfortunately always will. They influence a lot of my skeptical thinking.

I don't hold grudges if that is what you mean by forgiveness. I am not into emotional score keeping. Grudges upset my peace of mind. So I walk away from those who hurt me and do not let them live rent free in my mind.

I pity Karl. If he were not on his death bed, he probably would continue being a "good" SS soldier dutifully carrying out diabolical orders. Nor can I forgive Dylann Roof and the murderers of Betty Jane's sons. Making forgiveness a duty tells me that kind of forgiveness really doesn't come from the heart. Therefore, it is not real forgiveness. It is only self-seeking forgiveness so that "God" will forgive a person's trespasses. Instead, we need to eradicate evil, not forgive it.

Forgiveness is a difficult act to follow. Should a woman forgive her husband or boyfriend every time he abuses her and her children instead of placing charges against him with a restraining order? What would have happened if we forgave the Japanese for the bombing of Pearl Harbor? Should we have allowed them to continue to invade the US? Should the Japanese forgive us for dropping atomic bombs on Nagasaki and Hiroshima? Should we forgive terrorists for their savage acts of raping, maiming, enslaving, and killing? Should I forgive the person if he were to cut off my hands or forced my son to be a child soldier or my daughter a sex slave? Is such evil supposed to be forgiven? Not in my book.

I consider myself a good person, but I will not imitate Jesus' sacrifice on the cross or take up his mission. He was a good man causing no harm to anyone. In fact, his teachings and healings are quite remarkable and counter cultural. There are a lot of pretenders out in the world who claim to be doing things in Jesus' name. But most of them fail to live a sacrificial life and take up Jesus' cross and mission. Therefore, I think Jesus may be the real thing.

Before and since Jesus, empire building and power struggles continue unabated. Within the church, scandals, cruel dictatorial behavior by some in authority, spiritual pride, and an emphasis on private piety and afterlife salvation all destroy the faith of the innocent. Some governments and businesses exploit other countries' natural resources and their cheap labor pool.

Stock market manipulation by numerous financial people has destroyed millions of people's life's savings. Often bottom-line mentality leaves the ordinary workman helpless, unemployed, or under employed. This web of evil is more complicated than my enumeration just given.

Personally, since my beliefs are different from my girlfriend's parents, I have been ordered by them not to be in contact with her ever again. My heart is broken, but it will mend. I want no further relationships with pretenders who claim to be acting in God's name and best interest. Do I forgive them? No! Their daughter is a pawn in their hands; and I find their spiritual abuse, smug righteousness, pride, and lack of compassion unacceptable. They practice cruelty in the name of God. They are not the arm of God they think they are.

If she can't stand up to them now and come under my protection, our future with them in the picture would be one of psychological, spiritual, and emotional abuse. They are like the Inquisitors and I their victim. I haven't the power to stop them. And I will not sacrifice my own beliefs to appease them. So the next best thing is to leave the relationship forever. My death on their cross would accomplish nothing. That chapter in my life is closed. In time and with the help from Sarah and with my developing understanding about the Christian faith through our multi-faceted perspectives, I hope to be made whole. Thank you for your understanding and patience.

Anita's Thoughts: The heart of the gospel is forgiveness and love. Through belief in Jesus and his sacrifice on the cross, sinners believe their sins are forgiven. This forgiveness removes barriers between God and us and each other.

Seeking forgiveness for sins committed is the means for reestablishing this right relationship. Yet some victims find it impossible to forgive a perpetrator. And some perpetrators fail to seek forgiveness from their victims and God.

Also, those who sin and seek forgiveness with the intention of sinning again and again have not really repented.

As an ordained minister, I am called to preach the gospel and to proclaim God's love and forgiveness to repentant sinners. If I were called to Karl's bedside and heard about his horrific acts and his need for absolution, I could not and would not play God and absolve him of his sins and guilt. In fact, I do not believe I have the authority to do so considering the gravity of his sins and his timing for seeking forgiveness. Anything I would say would be meaningless, worthless, and cheap grace. God gives us life. We belong to God. And no one has any right to kill another person with the exception of self-defense.

I would encourage Karl to throw himself on God's mercy and justice and accept God's verdict. Karl reminds me of Constantine who became a Christian. Believing that Christian baptism would wipe away his sins, he was not baptized until just before his death. Contrary to that belief, I believe we are held accountable for our deeds and misdeeds in the present. We should repent of our sins of commission and omission. We need to seek forgiveness now from our victims and God instead of waiting for some magical eradication of sins at the time of death through baptism.

If I were Betty Jane's pastor, I would have suggested she visit her son's murderer in prison and to hear him out before making any decision to forgive him. If he were truly repentant, she could encourage the murderer to spend the rest of his life working out his penance amongst his fellow prisoners on behalf of the lives he took. Many religious people from outside the prisons have such a vocation. They try to save the souls of their fellow human beings. If her son's murderer were to accept this prison ministry and vocation, I am sure his repentance would help heal Betty Jane's broken heart and free her from any hatred, anger, revenge, and the burden to forgive. She would be like Jesus' mother, Mary, who watched the brutal death of her son on the cross. It was Jesus who asked God to forgive "them"—his executioners, the mob, and the religious and political establishment. Jesus appealed to God to forgive their sins and so should Betty Jane. Then she needs to "let go."

I find it hard to forgive unrepentant murderers such as Dylann Roof, the San Bernardino terrorists, and similarly crazed terrorists who pursue a misguided mission to kill and maim those they consider identifiable enemies that exist outside their hate dynasties. They are victims of insidious brainwashing who separate themselves from God and God's laws. They are taught by their leaders to worship a counterfeit god they believe requires them to carry out mayhem in his name against the lives of people outside their group, tribe, and race. Society needs to be protected from such evil. It is like a deadly cancer that destroys life. I cannot condone such evil. Nor am I required to forgive such evil. Our leaders have to decide how best to protect all people from such evil and eradicate it.

Jesus' first miracle in the Capernaum synagogue was the casting out of a demon from a person. He also cast out numerous demons residing in the Gerasene-possessed man. These demons were sent into a herd of about 2,000 swine which then ran off a cliff to their deaths. Must the same be done against all evil doers? If so, how will it affect our souls? I believe we need to pray for Dylann but that he needs to spend the rest of his life in jail. Terrorists need to be caught and imprisoned. Perhaps some form of Bishop Tutu's Truth and Reconciliation Commission needs to be established. However, I do not believe radical Islam and hate groups will repent and come to the table. Their sins are not only against people but also against God.

I do agree with the members of the Charleston Church that they need to let go of their hurt, anger, and hostilities in order to be delivered from the temptation of revenge and hate that can in turn lead to evil and bitterness.

As for my situation, I grew up in a large dysfunctional family and was subjected to self-righteous smugness and bullying. This behavior prepared me well for my adult life both as a teacher and a female minister. When confronted with narcissistic behavior on the part of different people who believed they had a position of importance, I soon learned that if I didn't play their game by their rules I would be sidelined, discredited, brow-beaten, ignored, humiliated, belittled, and mocked. These narcissists and bullies attempted to alienate people against me through lies and/or attacks on my character and capability. They rationalized the evil they did as a just cause—their cause. And as a woman, I had to be especially careful never to be in a man's presence alone. I insisted that men meet me in my office when my secretary or someone else was present.

I often wonder why narcissists and bullies feel threatened by me. Have I punctured their world and sense of equilibrium? Are they hypocritical Pharisees? Jesus told it like it was and not as they wanted it to be. I do likewise. I will not be someone's proxy or rubber stamp. Sincere acknowledgement and repentance for the evil these people have done and do never occurs. I think their pride and psychological problems prevent them from seeking forgiveness and repentance. All grounds for trust and reconciliation are absent. I refuse to be vindictive and fall into their sinful quagmire. I am always cordial but guarded when in their presence. Nor do I seek their company.

As a servant of our Lord Jesus, can I or should I forgive them when there is no repentance? Yes and no. I refuse to be their victim and to allow anger or resentment to exist in my mind and heart. I believe Jesus would not forgive them now or in the future unless they seek forgiveness and sincere repentance followed by good deeds. I turn their offenses over to God and pray that they will come to realize the evil they do and have done and will repent. It is their and God's decision. In the time left to me, I turn my efforts towards helping others and teaching them about the Christian faith. I pray that evil perpetrators will repent and stand up for truth, peace, justice, and love of neighbor in God's world.

Think About It

- Can you or do you agree with what others have written here? Why or why not? Be specific.
- Have any of your thoughts on forgiveness changed? How so?
- How can you overcome your reluctance to forgive?

Chapter 13

Reflections on Jesus' Final Words, Part II

Forgiveness: *Father, forgive them; for they do not know what they are doing.*[65]
Salvation: *Truly I tell you, today you will be with me in Paradise.*[66]
Relationship: *Woman, here is your son. Son, here is your mother.*[67]
Abandonment: *My God, my God, why have you forsaken me?*[68]
Agony: *I thirst.*[69]
Victory: *It is finished.*[70]
Reunion: *Father, into your hands I commend my spirit.*[71]

Anita: Our discussions on forgiveness raised many penetrating and unanswerable questions especially when applied to different real-life circumstances. In his first words from the cross, Luke's Greek verb indicates that Jesus repeatedly pleas for God to forgive "them." Jesus asks God not only to forgive the political/religious establishment and the Roman soldiers, but also his companions who desert him, Peter who denies knowing him, the fickle crowd that welcomes Jesus into Jerusalem and then turns against him. But I also believe he means us today.

Another example of forgiveness of enemies is told by Ernest Gordon in his book *Miracle on the River Kwai.*[72] During World War II, 12,000 Prisoners of War were put to building a railroad bridge for the Japanese. They were brutalized by their captors and underfed. Morale was low and hope was gone. Husky men were walking skeletons within weeks of their arrival at the prison camp. Two prisoners organized Bible study groups. Gordon writes,

> We ceased thinking about ourselves as victims of the same cruel jest and began to grasp the truth that suffering comes from human avarice and stupidity, not from God, and that the way out of suffering is through it, not avoiding it or denying its existence....
>
> Nowhere was the change in attitude more manifest than in our prayers. We learned to pray for others more than for ourselves. When we did pray for ourselves, it was not to get something, but to release some power within us.
>
> Gradually we learned to pray that hardest of all prayers: for our enemies....
>
> An incident that happened during the final months of imprisonment revealed to me how far we'd come from hatred.... A trainload of enemy soldiers pulled in. They were casualties from the fighting in Burma, and in pitiful plight: indescribably filthy, ragged, starving, their wounds full of maggots.
>
> My men's action was as instinctive as it was compassionate. With no order from me they moved over to clean the soldiers' wounds, give them our own ration of rice.... To our men, these were no longer enemies, but fellow sufferers.

Milton: That is an amazing story. In their hopeless, tragic situation, these POWs turned to God and became changed men. Their prayers and their relationship to God made all the difference.

Sarah: Viktor Frankl wrote a book entitled *Man's Search for Meaning.* In it, he writes about his and his fellow Jews' naked existence and horrific experiences in different Nazi concentration camps to which he was imprisoned. As a psychologist, he observed, conversed with, and analyzed why most men lost all hope in a possible future who then gave up on life with deadly consequences. Yet there were other men who tried to make meaning out of their daily tortures, who called upon their inner mental and spiritual resources and freedom to choose their action which no one could take from them. Many of these men had the strength to survive. Frankl writes:

> What was really needed was a fundamental change in our attitude toward life. We had to learn ourselves and, furthermore, we had to teach the despairing men, that *it did not really matter what we expected from life, but rather what life expected from us.* We needed to stop asking about the meaning of life, and instead to think of ourselves as those who were being questioned by life—daily and hourly. Our answer must consist, not in talk and meditation, but in right action and in right conduct. Life ultimately means taking the responsibility to find the right answer to its problems and to fulfill the tasks which it constantly sets for each individual.[73]

Anita: Thank you, Sarah. These parallel experiences of cruelly treated prisoners half a world apart demonstrate the importance of being the master of one's own mental and spiritual life. Jesus exhibits this same trait as he hung naked, brutally wounded, in excruciating pain, bleeding, abandoned, and dying on the cross between two thieves.

Jesus' only defender in this dire time is one of the thieves. He recognizes Jesus' innocence and goodness. Perhaps he is influenced by Jesus' repeated words of forgiveness for his persecutors. The thief probably wonders, "Why would a dying, crucified man, seek forgiveness for his persecutors?" Could the inscription of the charge against Jesus nailed over his head on the cross be true? Is Jesus "The King of the Jews?" Does the thief find God's reign in Jesus?

Mary: No doubt yes. This thief dares to ask Jesus to remember him when he comes into his kingdom. The thief had no reason to hope for a new life. He was a person of no account. But to Jesus, he matters. Jesus dies with him and opens heaven's gate for him by saying, "Truly I tell you, today you will be with me in Paradise." That tells me that the humble who align themselves with Jesus and his suffering find mercy and sanctuary with him in the life to come.

Anita: Jesus' third word refers to his relationship and love for his mother. He shows his concern for her when he tells her that John will now be her son and that she will be John's mother. This new relationship may represent the early formation of the Christian faith community.

Thomas: These words raise the question why can't his brothers and sisters take care of her.

Milton: It could be that they were not blood relatives. They may be Joseph's children from a prior marriage.

Mary: Or, at that time, they do not believe in Jesus' mission and who he is. They were not present at Jesus' crucifixion. But John is.

Anita: On a deeper level, Jesus shows concern for his mother and interpersonal relationships. He probably means that those in the faith community find their true family with each other.

Mary: How awful it is for Mary and thousands upon thousands of mothers whose children's death precedes their own. I think of today's refugees fleeing intolerable cruelty and war. Many of their children die in their flight and struggle to get to some safe harbor. I feel so helpless. Daily I cry and pray for these strangers. They are God's children caught in a vicious web of evil.

Thomas: I have to agree with you Mary. Why does such evil exist? Evil seems to have a life of its own.

Milton: At times, we all have these questions. I have always been challenged by Jesus' cry of despair and dereliction, "My God, my God, why have you forsaken me?" Am I to interpret that Jesus' life and work have been in vain?

Anita: Many of us at various times have experienced this hellish feeling of abandonment by God and others. This cry is one of ultimate spiritual, mental, and psychological suffering. It reflects the cries that many of us want to shout out to God from time to time but are reluctant to do so.

Many people's lives are savagely marked by suffering, incurable disease, broken homes, poverty, and all sorts of disequilibrium. Cries of lament are bold acts of faith, a faith that insists that the world must be experienced as it is lived. When we are stripped of everything, God is the only one to whom we can carry these outcries.

We bring our petitions to God with the resolute hope that God will hear and act.

Sarah: Yet our cries to God may be met with the silence of God. The silence of God and the darkness of our faith journey reveal to us that the world of faith often can be a world where there are no apparent answers, that sometimes life feels more like death, and that God seems more absent than present. Certainly many of the Jewish concentration prisoners felt that way.

Anita: Yes. Jesus feels totally alone in a hostile world. His disciples are hiding in fear for their lives. Abandonment is his final humiliation.

Sarah: No doubt Jesus identified with the psalmist in Psalm 22 which opens with these very same words—"My God, my God, why have you forsaken me?" All Jewish people know that by reciting the first line of a psalm that they have the entire psalm in mind. The three parties that show up in this lament are God, the sufferer, and the sufferer's enemies. This psalm moves back and forth from complaints, horrible doubt, and fear. It then moves to expressions of faith. It reminds me of an inscription found on the walls of a cellar in Cologne where Jews hid from the Nazis. "I believe in the sun, even when it is not shining. I believe in love, even when not feeling it. I believe in God, even when God is silent."

Jesus no doubt questions God's wisdom and why God has abandoned him. Gradually, Jesus' struggle of the soul eases and moves from utter hopelessness to the conviction that God has heard and will respond to his anguished cries.

Anita: I really like the inscription. It says it all. Like the psalmist, we can plead for God's help. We, as Jesus, need to trust God and God's wisdom. We need to ask ourselves whether we believe the crosses which we bear are a dead end or a purposeful breakthrough for Jesus and us. Our crosses seem to contradict the wisdom of the world.

Mary: It could be we need to pass through the valley with the shadows of death to reach new life. Psalm 23 follows Psalm 22 and reflects that understanding and is often read at funerals and during perilous times. Psalm 23 assures people that God is like a good shepherd that looks after our well-being. It also promises us eternal life where we will dwell in the house of the Lord forever.

Milton: Talk about crossing through the valley of death, some scholars believe Jesus was forced to walk through the streets of Jerusalem for three hours prior to his crucifixion. Jesus' crucifixion began at 9:00 a.m. He hung on the cross for six hours. His time on the cross was mercifully short in comparison to others who remain on their crosses for days. Thirst and dehydration overwhelm him.

Someone gives him a sponge full of sour wine on a hyssop branch. We could say that Jesus first drains the cup of wrath filled with God's divine reaction to evil. Through Jesus' sacrifice on the cross, his blood fills this emptied cup and becomes God's cup of blessing and cup of salvation. This cup reveals to us God's eternal love for us. On the cross, I believe Jesus conquers sin and death.

Anita: Jesus does not thirst for what the eye can see or the hand can grasp. Only with God will his thirst be satisfied. So Jesus says, "It is finished." It seems Jesus is reconciled to the importance of his work and self-giving. There is no anger or doubt. He goes from questioning God to trust and acceptance of God's wisdom. Now it is our turn to accept Jesus' life-giving gift and work.

With Jesus' last breath, he entrusts his spirit to God and returns home. "Father, into your hands I commend my spirit."

The light of the world goes out. The earth quakes. And the curtain in the Temple is torn in two. No longer will this curtain and the Temple priests deny people direct access to God. The old Temple is now obsolete. It is destroyed by the Romans in 70 CE.

Sarah: That may be so, but we Jews don't need a Temple to be with God. The theocracies of the high priests were corrupt in Jesus' day. As you know, a theocracy is a form of government that is ruled by religious leaders. Many people believe they are divinely inspired. I don't. Even today, there are theocracies such as in Iran where clerics, with the aid of the military, rule society. This spiritual abuse is forced upon the people and is not from God. Please remember, we Jews have our own covenant with God and access to God. The average Jew, then and today, cannot be held accountable for Jesus' death on the cross.

Anita: Well said. I agree with you. Joseph of Arimathea, a rich man and a dissenting member of the Sanhedrin regarding Jesus, goes to Pilate and gets permission to remove Jesus from the cross and bury him in his own tomb hewn out of rock. To be certain that Jesus is dead, "one of the soldiers pierced his side with a spear, and at once blood and water came out."[74] Joseph and his helpers undo Jesus from his cross and wrap him in a clean linen and lay him in Joseph's tomb. They then roll the huge stone in its trench to close the opening to the tomb. Jesus' women followers watch the burial and sealing of the tomb from afar.

Thomas: Is that the end of Jesus' life's story? A cross instead of a crown. Buried in a borrowed tomb.

Anita: The chief priests want to be sure it is the end of Jesus. They are afraid God will overrule them and their evil. So they go to Pilate and beg for a guard to be placed at his tomb.

> Sir, we remember what that impostor said while he was still alive, 'After three days I will rise again.' Therefore command

> the tomb to be made secure until the third day; otherwise his disciples may go and steal him away, and tell the people, 'He has been raised from the dead,' and the last deception would be worse than the first." Pilate said to them. "You have a guard of soldiers; go, make it as secure as you can." So they went with the guard and made the tomb secure by sealing the stone.[75]

Pilate and the chief priests fail to understand that no power can hold Jesus in a tomb if it is God's will.

But that is not the end of Jesus' story. The cross becomes a symbol for contradictions about God.

- Instead of a throne, Jesus has a cross.
- On the cross, Jesus is suspended between heaven and earth.
- Instead of subjects, Jesus has torturers.
- Instead of an authoritarian voice, Jesus is silenced.

The cross overturns the wisdom of every age and puts to shame any pride in human power.

- Jesus' suffering informs us that the way of the cross may be a path to suffering.
- Jesus values life, but it is worthless if we do not fight against evil within ourselves and evil within the world.
- The price of this fight against evil is not cheap. Jesus shows us the costliness of this struggle.
- Whether we are Jesus' followers or not, we all must pay the price for our position relevant to him.
- We cannot appreciate Jesus' suffering or interpret Calvary without first participating in it.
- The cross is a symbol of God's forgiveness for repentant sinners.

Think About It

- Can we look upon the three crosses as three different pathways we can and do take in life?
- Which cross do you choose?
- What are your thoughts about Jesus' family?
- Why did Jesus commend Mary to John's care?
- Have you ever felt complete abandonment by God? What was it like?
- Are you ready for your death?
- What is your interpretation regarding the symbolic meanings for the cross listed above?
- What GPS direction did the POWs, Nazi concentration camp Jews, Mary, Jesus, the chief priests, Pilate, and Joseph of Arimathea follow?

Chapter 14

The End is Just the Beginning

> *You will receive power when the Holy Spirit has come upon you; and you will be my witnesses in Jerusalem, in all Judea and Samaria, and to the ends of the earth.*
>
> Acts 1:8

Anita: Joseph of Arimathea and his men bury Jesus in Joseph's new tomb. They secure it. Women watch from a distance. Then the chief priests post a guard at the tomb. Jesus' enemies want to be sure that he cannot rise from the dead. They fail.[76]

At dawn on the first day of the week, several women disciples of Jesus go to his tomb carrying spices for his body. There were no guards present, and they found the stone rolled back. They find no body in the tomb. They are dumbfounded. What has happened? Then two men in dazzling clothes appear to them. They ask the women why they are looking for the living among the dead. The women can't give an answer. Who rolled the stone aside? Did these men or someone else steal Jesus' body? The women stand their ground unafraid and want answers. The men tell them that Jesus has risen from the dead as earlier foretold by him. Then they remember Jesus' words but still do not understand.

They run from the tomb to tell the eleven apostles what has happened. The apostles don't believe the women. But just to be sure, Peter and others run to the tomb to verify whether their report about the disappearance of Jesus' body is true. They go home amazed and perplexed at what has happened. Should they believe what the men told the women? How can Jesus be risen from the dead and alive?

On that same day, two of Jesus' disillusioned and devastated disciples travel with heavy hearts on the road to Emmaus. For three years, their expectations about Jesus were the glue that held his disciples and followers together. Many gave up everything to be with him. They had looked to Jesus for liberation, value, and security. When Jesus is crucified and dies, they become unglued. Their hopes turn to despair. Grief and darkness overwhelm them.

Milton: It easy to understand their feelings. How often do we start a new venture with the same high hopes Jesus' disciples may have had. We believe all will go well for us and that God is with us. Who then can be against us? Then slowly but surely we begin to realize expectations do not turn out as anticipated. Also, those friends upon whom we counted one by one give some lame excuse for being unable to help us. In defeat, we slowly turn our backs on our high hopes.

Anita: On the road to Emmaus, these disciples encounter a stranger who is Jesus but their mind's eye keeps them from recognizing him. He asks them what they are discussing. "Then one of them, whose name was Cleopas, answered him:

> "Are you the only stranger in Jerusalem who does not know the things that have taken place there in these days?" He asked them, "What things?" They replied, "The things about Jesus of

> Nazareth, who was a prophet mighty in deed and word before God and all the people, and how our chief priests and leaders handed him over to be condemned to death and crucified him. But we had hoped that he was the one to redeem Israel.
>
> Yes, and besides all this, it is now the third day since these things took place. Moreover, some women of our group astounded us. They were at the tomb early this morning, and when they did not find his body there, they came back and told us that they had indeed seen a vision of angels who said that he was alive. Some of those who were with us went to the tomb and found it just as the women had said; but they did not see him."
>
> Then he said to them, "Oh, how foolish you are, and how slow of heart to believe all that the prophets have declared! Was it not necessary that the Messiah should suffer these things and then enter into his glory?" Then beginning with Moses and all the prophets, he interpreted to them the things about himself in all the scriptures.[77]

Thomas: So what scripture is Jesus referring to?

Anita: It appears in Isaiah II 52:11-53:12. Isaiah II lived during the time of the Jewish exile in Babylon. It was he who said that the Jewish people should be a light to the world so as to bring all peoples to God. Their suffering was to be an example of suffering without remorse for sins they committed before defeat and exile. Jewish people's hopes are to spring out of their despair. Israel as a nation was to be God's Suffering Servant. Through the Servant's sufferings, God will reconcile or win over to a friendly attitude the peoples of the world to Godself.

Isaiah believed that someone or Israel as a nation would redeem or restore all nations to this right relationship with

God. This person or collective group became known as God's Suffering Servant. Early Christians came to believe that Jesus was this Suffering Servant.

A divine speaker tells us:

> See, my servant shall prosper; he shall be exalted and lifted up, and shall be very high. Just as there were many who were astonished at him—so marred was his appearance, beyond human semblance, and his form beyond that of mortals—so he shall startle many nations; kings shall shut their mouths because of him; for that which had not been told them they shall see, and that which they had not heard they shall contemplate.[78]

Spectators then ask:

> Who has believed what we have heard? And to whom has the arm of the Lord been revealed? For he grew up before him like a young plant, and like a root out of dry ground; he had no form or majesty that we should look at him; nothing in his appearance that we should desire him. He was despised and rejected by others; a man of suffering and acquainted with infirmity; and as one from whom others hide their faces he was despised, and we held him of no account.[79]

Milton: I think it is important we remember that one way God reveals Godself and communicates with us is through Jesus, the prophets, and scripture. Early Christians accepted the Hebrew Scriptures as their own. They read the Old Testament from their perspective of Jesus as the risen Lord. So when they began to re-read the Old Testament, many prophecies that were given there assumed an entirely different meaning.

The Old Testament then is interpreted by the New Testament, and the New Testament is understood through the

Old Testament. The New Testament fulfills the prophecies of the Old Testament, but the New Testament does not replace or destroy the Old. So we see the fulfillment of some of Isaiah II's prophecies with the person of Jesus.

Thomas: How?

Milton: Jesus is lifted up on a cross. Spectators watched, mocked, jeered or cried. The end of Jesus' life was one of suffering and rejection by his opponents and many of the same people he helped. Jesus was counted of no significance to the religious and political leaders of his day. Jesus experienced painful loneliness.

Sarah: In Isaiah 53:4-5, astonished converts speak and confess that something new has happened, a new reality has happened.

Thomas: How so?

Sarah: In the ancient world those who suffered were believed to be smitten by God. Yet this Suffering Servant has been exalted by God. Isaiah 40 begins with the call for the servant to comfort the people. Now the final order is given by God for the Jewish people to leave Babylon, to leave their exile and the splendid city of Babylon, and the land of pagan gods. God wants Israel to have and maintain a special identity as God's light in this world, an identity untainted by paganism.

The Servant becomes the sacrificial lamb who carries away people's sins and infirmities. The Jewish world view of suffering changes.

> Surely he has borne our infirmities and carried our diseases; yet we accounted him stricken, struck down by God, and afflicted. But he was wounded for our transgressions, crushed for our iniquities; upon him was the punishment that made us whole, and by his bruises we are healed.[80]

No longer will the afflicted or sick be considered sinners who are out of favor with God. When this scripture says the Suffering Servant was wounded for our transgressions, Isaiah means that the Servant bears peoples' sins.

Thomas: What do you mean when you say the Servant bear's peoples' sins?

Sarah: To bear peoples' sins means to endure the consequences of their sins which is death. Before the appearance of this Servant, people tried to make themselves right with God by touching an unblemished animal before it was sacrificed. They believed that animal carried away their sin. The animal's death was a blood substitution for the death caused by their sin. As we said earlier, we get the word scapegoat from this practice.

Sin separates people from God. True happiness cannot be found outside of God. Therefore, the Servant bears the consequences for the sins of the Babylonian exiles' parents. It was their parents' failure to fulfill their part of their covenant with God that caused their defeat and exile. Not only did the parents suffer but also their children for their parents' sins.

Anita: In the same way, Jesus took upon himself others peoples' sins and endured the consequences for their sins.

In Isaiah 53:9, the Servant dies with common criminals and is buried in a rich man's tomb.

The positive effects of Jesus' suffering are prefigured in Isaiah 53:10-12. Isaiah says that it was the will of God that the Servant suffers to show God's judgment against sin and God's mercy upon sinful humanity. From the New Testament perspective, Jesus becomes the Suffering Servant who made his life an offering for sin.

Thomas: Which means?

Anita: Jesus as the Servant took our punishment for our sins. He wiped our sins away by his sacrificial death. He is exalted by God. Christians vicariously identify and suffer with Jesus. Making amends for sins comes only through submission, obedience, exile and return to God. What is astonishing to Jews and to the followers of Jesus is that God has never before been revealed in weakness.

Thomas: Why would God prefer to be revealed to us through weakness?

Anita: Probably because God does not want to overpower us. God chooses not to intervene directly in human affairs but has decided to work through the prophets and God's servants.

The Jewish people's suffering comes to an end in Babylon, but it will not be the end of their suffering in world history. All kinds of atrocities by pagans and Christians have been perpetrated against them. Yet they still endure as a people and as God's Suffering Servant.

Mary: The same may be said for Christian martyrs and those Christians who deny themselves, pick up their cross, and follow Jesus.

Anita: Yes. When all these things happen, God restores the Suffering Servant and places him among the great. The same can be said of Jesus whose life and death are vindicated by his resurrection.

Our travelers on the road to Emmaus urge the stranger walking with them to stay with them. He does. And at table, the stranger took bread, blessed it, broke it and gave it to them. Then their eyes were opened, and they realize that it was Jesus who opened scripture to them. Then Jesus vanishes.

The two men immediately return to Jerusalem to tell everyone that Jesus appeared to them and what he had taught them. When they arrive, the disciples have exciting news as well. They tell them that Jesus has appeared to Peter. In their excitement, Jesus appears to all of them. Fear and doubt grip them. Are they seeing a ghost? Jesus asks them to touch him and to see his wounds. No, he is not a ghost. He asks for something to eat and is given a piece of broiled fish which he takes and eats in their presence.

> Then he opened their minds to understand the scriptures, and he said to them. Thus it is written, that the Messiah is to suffer and to rise from the dead on the third day, and that repentance and forgiveness of sins is to be proclaimed in his name to all nations, beginning from Jerusalem. You are witnesses of these things. And see, I am sending upon you what my Father promised; so stay here in the city until you have been clothed with power from on high.[81]

Milton: You forgot to mention that after Jesus' resurrection, the guards went to the chief priests and reported what happened. The priests and elders bribe the guards in exchange for their testimony that while they were asleep Jesus' disciples stole his body.[82]

Thomas: I doubt that tale carried much weight. The rolling back of the stone alone would awaken the guards. But the truth of the matter will never be known exactly how Jesus rose from the dead.

Mary: You are right. But there can be no denying that Jesus did rise from the dead because he appeared to hundreds of people.

Anita: Yes. Our knowledge of what happened in the immediate years following the death and resurrection of Jesus comes from the entire New Testament, including the gospels, Acts, and letters written by various apostles and disciples. All these documents were written well after the death of Jesus. We also have information from other sources such as legal documents of the time and from the church historian Eusebius and his book *The History of the Church from Christ to Constantine.* Eusebius was born about 260 CE. He had access to numerous documents which he meticulously recorded and which no longer exist today.

The author of the Gospel of Luke and the Book of Acts is believed to have been a second-generation Christian who knew people who had first-hand experiences of Jesus. He participated in the life of the emerging new faith community known as the Christian Community. The author could have been the Greek physician, Luke, who accompanied Paul on his missionary journeys. The second half of the Book of Acts could have been his travel diary.

Some scholars believe Luke/Acts were written before Nero torched Rome in 64 CE who blamed the fire on the Christians. This fire happened before the Jewish uprising. In 70 CE, Jerusalem was destroyed by Roman General Titus and his army. Because these events are missing from Luke/Acts, scholars date these writings before 60 CE. Other scholars, such as Luke Timothy Johnson, date these books at a much later date.

Luke's purpose in writing Luke/Acts was to show to Theophilus, a Roman official, and the larger world, the divine origins and progression of the Christian movement, to awaken faith in others, and to dismiss charges against Christians that they (Christians) were destructive of Jewish institutions and a danger to the security of the Roman Empire.

Milton: May I mention here that Luke's accounts are not history as we know and understand history today. Instead they are faith documents that help reveal God's mighty acts in history and God's open-ended plan for our salvation.

Anita: That's true. God in Jesus and in the Holy Spirit are the forces that inspire and move the disciples into action. They call people then and now into a faith community and to a new way of living and dying. The risen Jesus tells the disciples to wait until they are clothed in power from on high.

Thomas: Which is?

Anita: The Holy Spirit that empowers, leads, and guides them. Remember, the Holy Spirit is God's invisible presence with us.

Thomas: So what will the disciples do in the meantime?

Anita: They are not prepared to do anything but wait, pray, and study anew the Old Testament scripture from their new perspective. Also, they elect by casting lots a replacement for Judas. Matthias is chosen.

Milton: Those men who were part of Jesus' inner circle were known as *apostles.* There were 12 apostles who symbolically represented the 12 tribes of Israel. The church will eventually become known as the New Israel.

Mary: The *disciples* are followers of Jesus who were not part of Jesus' inner circle and who did not devote their entire lives to carrying forward Jesus' ministry.

Milton: However, Paul claims he is an apostle of Jesus even though he did not know Jesus before his conversion. Paul continually seeks to be part of Jesus' inner circle even though the apostles reluctantly accept him.

Anita: On the day of Pentecost, the Holy Spirit descends upon about 120 followers of Jesus who are gathered together.

> Suddenly from heaven there came a sound like the rush of a violent wind, and it filled the entire house where they were sitting. Divided tongues, as of fire, appeared among them,

> and a tongue rested on each of them. All of them were filled with the Holy Spirit and began to speak in other languages, as the Spirit gave them ability.[83]

Wind, fire, and smoke are all signs of God's presence. The stir caused by this experience attracts the attention of Jews—those from Jerusalem and Jewish pilgrims who came from afar to celebrate this religious holiday.

The astonished crowd accuses Jesus' disciples of drunkenness. Peter takes charge and speaks to the assembled multitude. He declares they are not drunk and that what is happening was prophesied by the prophet Joel. Peter also says that when God pours out the Holy Spirit, it is a sign that the Last Days of God's kingdom has arrived. This new era will be a time when God's rule reigns and when the crucified and resurrected Jesus will judge the living and the dead.

Peter, like the prophets of old, urgently calls the people to

> Repent, and be baptized...in the Name of Jesus Christ so that your sins may be forgiven; and you will receive the gift of the Holy Spirit. For the promise is for you, for your children, and for all who are far away, everyone whom the Lord our God calls to him.[84]

About 3,000 people, mostly Jews, are baptized on Pentecost. They devote themselves to the apostles' teachings, worship in the Temple, and live communally where everyone shares everything in common. From that time on, Pentecost is celebrated as the birthday or first day in the life of the church.

Milton: Peter has come into his own. He knows that Jesus forgives him for denying him. Peter plans never to waver and falter again. He is no longer a timid, frightened man. He is now an assertive leader filled with the Holy Spirit.

Anita: That's true. One day, Peter and John are on their way to pray in the Temple when a lame beggar from birth calls out to them for money. Peter says:

> I have no silver or gold, but what I have I give you; in the name of Jesus Christ of Nazareth, stand up and walk.[85]

The beggar's feet and ankles are made strong. He then stands. He is so excited that he runs and jumps with glee. He attracts the attention of a large crowd. The crowds wonder how this miracle occurred.

Peter takes this opportunity to address the crowd. He speaks of their collective guilt in the killing of Jesus, God's anointed. He recognizes that they acted in ignorance when they did not heed the prophets who foretold the people about Jesus' coming to his people. If they repent and receive Jesus as their Savior, they will be saved. Otherwise, they will be lost forever.

The plot thickens. Another 5,000 repent and convert on this day in front of the Temple because of Peter's and John's preaching and their ability to heal in Jesus' name.

The Temple authorities are enraged that Peter and John are preaching that Jesus rose from the dead and that they blame the Sanhedrin for Jesus' death. The Temple guards arrest both men. That day and night Peter and John spend in prison.

The next day they stand before the Sanhedrin unafraid. Peter and John proclaim bold new religious beliefs. They say that salvation is only through Jesus. God has not and will not send anyone else to save them. Nor will adherence to the Law save them. Only faith in Jesus Christ will save people.

The Sanhedrin and most Jewish people at that time believed that they will be saved through strict adherence to the Law of Moses.

Milton: Adherence to the Law versus faith is a source of tension between religious groups then and now.

Anita: The Sanhedrin orders Peter and John never to speak or talk about Jesus again. Peter's boldness causes him to defy the Sanhedrin and say they will obey God only and not them. A revolution begins. The men are released. They praise God and pray for more boldness.

Repeated beatings and imprisonments by Temple authorities occur. On one occasion, Gamaliel, a respected and famous Pharisee, cautions the Sanhedrin that if this Jesus movement is from God, they will not be able to stop it.[86]

Think About It:

- How does Jesus fulfill the Suffering Servant's role?
- Why would adherence to the Law not be sufficient to be accepted by God?
- Why do Peter and John tell the esteemed religious authorities of their time that salvation is only through Jesus?
- What do you think is the meaning of salvation?
- Have you experienced God's presence? Do you wish to share that experience?
- Have you ever had a road to Emmaus experience? What was it like?
- How do you account for the founding of the Christian movement?
- Who in recent history is God's Suffering Servant?
- How does God speak to you today?

Chapter 15

The Emerging Church, Part I

You call for faith:
I show you doubt, to prove that faith exists.
The more of doubt, the stronger faith, I say,
If faith o'ercomes doubt.

Bishop Blougram's Apology
Robert Browning

Anita: When Christianity began during the first century, there were more Jewish people living outside Israel than inside the nation. Many of them were driven into exile by the conquering Assyrians (722 BCE) and Babylonians (586 BCE). These Jews were called Diaspora Jews because they settled in lands outside of Judah and Israel and yet maintained their Jewish identity.

After Alexander the Great conquered the known world (334 BCE), Greek culture dominated the Middle East and had a great influence on Diaspora Jews. They spoke Greek and/or the language of their adopted country. Many were no longer able to read their scripture in Hebrew or Aramaic so they had them translated into Greek. This work became known as the Septuagint.

You will remember that on Pentecost, the day Jesus' disciples were filled with the Holy Spirit, Diaspora Jews from various countries were in Jerusalem celebrating the end of the barley harvest and the beginning of the wheat harvest known by the Jews as Pentecost. Many of these Diaspora Jews were Greek speaking and were converted to Christianity on that day.

Those Jews who converted to Christianity became known as Jewish Christians and a sect within Judaism. They remained Jews by birth and lineage.

Non-Diaspora Jews and Diaspora Jews who were converted to Christianity lived communally. Even though all these people were one in Jesus Christ, language and cultural differences created friction between the two groups.

The Non-Diaspora Jewish Christians kept many of their long-standing customs. One such custom was the collection of alms every Friday morning to be distributed later in the day to the needy. Those Christians who had no means of support received a weekly ration of food.

Many Aramaic-speaking Jewish Christians felt superior to the Hellenistic Christian Jews. This attitude manifested itself in unequal food and alms distribution. To resolve this problem and with the approval of both factions, seven Greek-speaking Jews were appointed to oversee the welfare and distribution of alms and food to their people. Stephen was one of the seven.

These early Jewish Christians worshiped in the Temple and in their local synagogues. All Jewish Christians looked upon themselves as a separate branch of Judaism and not as a new and separate religion. Trouble broke out between Jewish believers and Jewish Christians. Each sect was intolerant of the other group and often debated the merits of their belief.

Hellenistic Jewish Christians were the most controversial. Among the seven, Stephen proved to be a dynamic speaker full of the Holy Spirit. His vision of God and the direction of the faith community was considerably different from non-Christian Jews. So he engaged in debates in the synagogues where lay people could preach and argue their point of view. Some Jews charged Stephen with blasphemy and brought him before the Sanhedrin and the high priest. Stephen charged them with betraying God and recounted Jewish history to them. Then he gazed into heaven and said he saw Jesus standing at the right hand of God.[87]

Milton: Stephen also believed that the day of the Temple and its customs were over. He said Jesus had superseded the need for the Temple as God does not dwell in anything made by the hands of people. The Sanhedrin men covered their ears. Then in their rage and without a trial, they dragged Stephen out of the city and stoned him. With his dying breath, Stephen cried out to God to forgive them. Saul watched and approved of this killing.[88]

Anita: From that time on, Saul of Tarsus becomes a pivotal figure in the emerging church. He is a Diaspora Pharisee who came from Tarsus, located in modern-day Turkey's southwestern coast, to study the Law under the famous teacher Gamaliel who sat on the Sanhedrin.

Saul's anger and defense of the Jewish faith cause him to take on the role of the Sanhedrin's policeman. He vows to stop the teachings of the Jewish Christians. He will not accept their teachings that the crucified Jesus had risen from the dead and now was the Living Lord prophesied as Israel's long-awaited Messiah. The Book of Acts informs us "that day a severe persecution began against the church in Jerusalem, and all, except the apostles, were scattered throughout the countryside of Judea and Samaria....Now those who were scattered went from place to place, proclaiming the word."[89]

Paul asks for and receives authority from Temple officials the power to arrest, imprison, and put to death all Christians. He targets Damascus, Syria.

Milton: Even though Damascus is not under the political jurisdiction of the rulers of Judea, the Temple leaders and the Romans worked out an agreement whereby the Temple leaders' authority extends to all Jews within the Roman Empire. Therefore, Saul's letters of authority by the Temple leaders were death and/or imprisonment warrants for the Christian Jews. Christians living in Damascus had heard about Saul and feared him.

Anita: Let me show you the first of a three-part video series that helps to illustrate first century religious and cultural Jewish thinking regarding the early Christians. It begins with two elderly Jewish friends, Samuel and Nathan, who are diaspora Jews. They meet each other in the marketplace in Tarsus. The year is 80 CE.

***

"Hello Nathan! What brings you to Tarsus? It has been years since we have seen each other. Don't you now live in Rome?"

"It is good to see you Samuel. How many years has it been anyway? Let me think. The last time we saw each other was after Saul converted to Christianity. Remember?"

"Indeed I do. He got up one day in our synagogue to tell us of his fantastic experience. He tried to convince us that we, too, should become Christians. Many of us wanted to stone him to death. But since he was one of us, we just booed him and pushed him out of the synagogue. We warned him never to step foot in the synagogue again or we would stone him to death."

"You know, Samuel, I saw Saul several years ago in Rome and had many meetings with him. He told me of his beliefs and why he became a Christian. That was before the great fire in Rome in 64. Then I lost track of him."

"Nathan, how long will you be in Tarsus?"

"About one week."

"Will you break bread with me tonight? I would love to learn more about what you know of Saul and his new beliefs. Will sunset be all right with you?"

"That will be fine."

***

"Nathan, now that I have told you how we are doing here in Tarsus, tell me whatever happened to Saul."

"Well, do you remember how he told us about encountering the living Jesus of Nazareth, who was crucified, dead, buried, and then rose from the dead and had become Saul's Lord and Savior?"

"It has been so many years. I do not remember everything. All I know is that he had crossed all bounds acceptable to us Jews."

"Saul told me what happened to him and how it changed his entire life. He was on the road to Damascus with letters from the Temple leaders which gave him authority to arrest any Jew in the city who believed in this Jesus of Nazareth. On this road, a light from heaven flashed around him. He fell to the ground and heard a voice say to him, 'Saul, Saul, why do you persecute me? Saul asked, 'Who are you Lord?' And the voice replied, 'I am Jesus, whom you are persecuting. But get up and enter the city, and you will be told what you are to do.'"[90]

"The men who were with Saul heard a voice too, but saw nothing. When Saul got up from the ground, he was blind. He had to be led into Damascus by those men who were with him. He neither ate nor drank anything for three days."

"Nathan, I wonder what was going through his mind during that time."

"I think he was in a state of shock. Over and over again he asked himself how Jesus could be alive. He was crucified and put in a grave. Dead men do not rise from the dead—at least not until the Messiah comes. Then Saul told me about Ananias, a Christian, whom Jesus ordered in a vision to go to Saul to restore his sight. Ananias said, 'Brother Saul, the Lord Jesus, who appeared to you on your way here, has sent me so that you may regain your sight and be filled with the Holy Spirit.'"

"Ananias did not want to go to Saul because he knew what Saul's mission was. But Ananias told Saul that Jesus told him that he had chosen Saul to bring his name before Gentiles and kings and before the people of Israel. And that he, Jesus, will show Saul how much he must suffer for the sake of Jesus' name."[91]

"Samuel, do you remember how strong willed Saul was? He always wanted everything his way. For the first time in his life, he said he had to wait for the Lord's word and will."

"That's nonsense Nathan. Do you really believe this happened to him?"

"Yes, Saul is not the person we knew as boys. He uses his great mind to convince others that they need to be converted to Jesus the Messiah to be restored to a right relationship with God. He believes the Law and legalism fail in this regard."

"Nonsense Nathan. I remember hearing reports that after Saul's sight was restored he preached in Damascus, in the synagogues, and on street corners. Our religious authorities there sought to kill him. But somehow he escaped."

"Saul told me that some Christians lowered him in a basket over the city walls at night so that he could escape from being murdered. By the way, after Saul was baptized he changed his name to Paul to show that he was a changed man, a transformed man, a new man. He vowed that he would start his life over. Instead of persecuting Jesus' followers, he would spread Jesus' message to all who would listen to him."

"Nathan, where did he go after his escape from Damascus? He must have been a wanted man by then."

"He told me he went to Arabia for some quiet time with God. He needed time to rethink his faith and the new life that lay ahead. Paul prayed for guidance, strength and moral courage for the overwhelming task God had set before him. After a time in Arabia, he began his missionary work in spreading the gospel message among the Jews and Gentiles. Then he went to Jerusalem to visit with Jesus' apostles Peter, James, and John. Another 14 years passed before Paul returned to Jerusalem. This time he took Titus, a Greek convert, with him. By that time, Paul defended the right of Gentile Christians not to be circumcised. Reluctantly the council agreed that pagan converts did not need to be circumcised."[92]

"These Christians ought to be barred from the Temple and synagogues. They drag us down with them. Everywhere they go they stir up trouble. And we have enough trouble with Rome already. Surely you have heard what they say about them?"

"Yes, Samuel. I have heard many things. But some of the things people say about the Christians are so ridiculous that no right-thinking person should believe them."

"Why the Christians are cannibals and eat babies when they secretly gather together."

"I asked Paul about this rumor. He said it was untrue and that they get together to remember Jesus' Last Supper with his disciples. They share a common loaf of bread and a common cup of wine in remembrance of him."

"O.K. But isn't it true that the Christians do not like people who refuse to accept their new belief and that is why they set fire to Rome?"

"Samuel, these Christians are good people. I know that now. They would not hurt anyone. In fact, they save unwanted Gentile babies whose fathers put them out in front of their houses or outside the city gates. These pagan fathers don't care whether their children live or die. The Christians adopt these babies and care for them. As for the fire, I believe that crazy Emperor Nero torched Rome. He wanted a new and more beautiful Rome. He thought he could burn the slums and the poor people in them all at the same time and blame the fire on Christians."

"Well, you may be right on that. Nero was a crazy man. But I hear these Christians worship the head of a donkey."

"Samuel, someone did scratch a picture and message on a wall in Rome. I saw it. It looked like the work of a child who didn't know the meaning of what he was drawing and writing. Christians worship an invisible God and the same God we worship."

"I doubt that. I hear these Christians worship many gods. Saul or Paul knows there is only one God. As soon as we Jews are able to speak, we say—'Hear, O Israel: The Lord is our God, the Lord alone. You shall love the Lord your God with all your heart, and with all your soul, and with all your might.'[93] How can Paul believe in this Jesus as though he were a god?"

"Your question was the exact same question I put to Saul. And he said that Jesus is God in the flesh, God incarnate. I wrote down his words and carry them with me. He has an interesting understanding about God that has intrigued me. Here, let me get it out and read to you what he says.

> Christ is the image of the invisible God, the firstborn of all creation; for in Christ all the things were created, in heaven and on earth, visible and invisible, whether thrones or dominions or principalities or authorities—all things were created through Christ and for Christ. Christ is before all things, and in Christ all things hold together. Christ is the head of the body, the church; Christ is the beginning, the first born from the dead that in everything Christ might be preeminent. For in Christ all the fullness of God was pleased to dwell, and through Christ all things are reconciled to God, whether on earth or in heaven, making peace by the blood of Christ's cross.[94]

What do you think?"

"Why, that's blasphemous."

"That is what I thought when I first heard it. But then Paul explained what he meant."

"Nathan, you sound as though you are a Christian carrying around Saul's words. Are you?"

"Let me explain what his words mean. No one has seen God and lived. Yet Paul says that Jesus is the image or manifestation of what God is like. Jesus represents God in human form so that through him we can understand what God is like."

"Don't you know Nathan that our Law forbids our associating with someone like Jesus? God cannot be like Jesus. He associated with beggars, prostitutes, drunkards, tax collectors, and even Gentiles. God made us the chosen people. We are to avoid all contact with unclean people and Gentiles. How can God be like Jesus?"

"Hear me out Samuel. Paul believes this Jesus is God in human form. Jesus was present and part of God at the beginning of the world. When Paul says that Jesus is the firstborn of all creation, he means he is the Messiah. All creation should give their highest honors to him. God is in Jesus who created this world, and the entire world should have Jesus as their goal."

"Nathan, you are beginning to irritate me. Jesus was nothing more than a simple carpenter with grand ideas. Oh, I have to admit that many of his pronouncements had to be made. He was bright and analyzed the state of our spiritual lives. His attack on the religious authorities in Jerusalem also was justified. Those prancing and parading religious leaders with their false piety sickened many of us. Their rule was as harsh and as unreasonable as the Romans, maybe even more so. But the simple truth Jesus represented and his stand against the religious authorities doesn't make him the Messiah or, as the Greeks would say, the Christ."

"Listen Samuel, Paul says that Jesus is the head of the Christian faith community known as the church. The church is not a building but is made up of the lives of believers who recognize only Jesus as their Lord. It is the risen Jesus who breathes life into church members through God's Holy Spirit. These people now represent Jesus. Jesus is supreme in everything. He was part of God before the creation. Through his resurrection, he demonstrated that he conquered death and sin."

"Why would God do such a crazy thing as to come in the flesh as a humble carpenter and let himself be crucified?"

"How else could God reveal to us how easily we can sin and overlook what is important in life? In the past, we have silenced or killed our prophets. And in recent history, Herod had John the Baptist's head cut off. Look at how easy it is for Rome to execute innocent people. Romans are a godless people who worship and deify their emperors. God wanted us Jews to show the world how God desired us to live. But what did we do? We kept the Law and knowledge of God to ourselves and from the Gentiles."

"That is not entirely true Nathan. We have always allowed Gentiles to convert to Judaism so long as they are circumcised and observe our Law and dietary regulations."

"Yes, yes! I know that. But were we more concerned about the letter of the Law and enforcement of it more than the Spirit of the Law? Is it not possible that Jesus came to free us from blind obedience to a legalism devoid of love? Are we not meant to live by the Spirit of the Law?

"Nathan, you are wandering off the subject. How does Jesus reconcile people to God? What does he mean?"

"God in Jesus came to us in love. Through Jesus' death, God is saying that God loves us enough to allow Jesus to suffer and die for us. The cross tells us that God will stop at nothing to win our love. God's love through Jesus assures us that God accepts us. The cross also tells us that suffering and death can happen to God's people. We Jews always thought that sinners are the ones who suffer. Jesus says that rain falls on the fields of the wicked as well as on the fields of the good. Jesus' cross tells us that good health and prosperity are no assurance of God's blessings."

"It is getting late. I will think about what you have said tonight. Nathan, can we meet tomorrow evening and continue this conversation?"

"Yes Samuel, Shalom."

"Shalom."

***

Thomas: Well, this video may explain a little of what went on in the early church. But I have problems with Paul's conversion and imprinting his brand of Christianity on the early church. He did not even know Jesus. So how could he speak for Jesus?

Sarah: I agree with you Thomas. We Jews agree with Samuel's position.

Milton: But you could say that God called Paul similar to the way God called prophets for a special purpose. God chose Paul to spread Jesus' message to the world.

Thomas: But where is Paul's free will? He had to be blinded in order to get his cooperation in becoming an advocate for the early church.

Anita: That's true. But consider the fact that Paul was zealous on God's behalf before his conversion. The Christian faith has its roots in Judaism. Paul was on a mission but on the wrong track until Jesus interceded. Christians believe that Jesus is the light of the world. Perhaps that is why Paul was blinded before he could see the light. Jesus came to show us God's love and forgiveness of sin. He wants to turn hearts of stone into hearts that love one another that lead them to God's eternal home.

Edward: Well, that is a commendable vision regarding who Jesus is. But who really speaks for God. Paul's letters are often authoritarian and seem to put in place a new Law that creates misinterpretations about God's purposes.

Mary: But there needs to be guidance and a moral structure in place or people will break boundaries and will commit all kinds of sins not only sexually but in their interpersonal relationships.

Anita: Paul also condemns and sets down boundaries regarding people's sense of superiority and competition for power over others. But let me ask you whether religious leaders should impose their will over others that have different beliefs?

Thomas: Absolutely not. Remember my struggles with my girlfriend and her parents. It is tyranny of the worse kind. Take for instance the radical Islamists who kill, rape, behead, enslave, imprison, and torture non Islamists as though they are God's enemy. Paul was doing some of the same things to Jewish Christians. I want nothing to do with a god that sanctions these deeds. Frankly, I believe the Islamists terrorist's god is of their own invention so that they can justify their evil actions.

Anita: Thank you all for your thoughts. It is time for us to break for today. At our next meeting, we will continue to look at Paul's influence on the early church.

Think About It

- Why do people try to impose their beliefs on people who have different beliefs?
- Give examples in today's world where this behavior occurs.
- What are your thoughts on religious leaders who authorize executions, imprisonment, and/or whippings toward people who are unconverted to their way of believing?
- How do they justify their position?
- Why do you agree or disagree with Samuel or Nathan?

Chapter 16

The Emerging Church, Part II

Do you not know that your body is a temple of the Holy Spirit within you, which you have from God, and that you are not your own; you were bought with a price; therefore glorify God in your body.

1 Cor. 6:19-20

Anita: At our last meeting, we discussed the difference between Diaspora and non-Diaspora Jews and how they fell under the jurisdiction of the Jerusalem Temple and Paul's role as part of the Temple's law enforcement before his conversion. Then we watched a video where two childhood friends of Paul meet after many years in the marketplace in Tarsus, Paul's hometown. They meet one evening to discuss Paul's conversion and campaign to spread the good news about Jesus.

Today we will view the second part of this video series to learn more about the controversies between Jews and Christians in the first century.

***

"Shalom! Nathan!"

"Shalom! Samuel!"

"Come Nathan. Sit here beside me. Tonight my wife and daughter want to join us. They wish to listen to and be part of our conversation. I told them what we discussed last night, and they want to learn more about Saul. I mean, Paul."

"Here they are now. Let me introduce Rachel, my wife, and Mary, my daughter."

"It is my pleasure to meet both of you."

"It is our pleasure as well."

"I find it interesting that you want to learn more about Paul, Samuel's and my childhood friend. Paul has had an interesting life. He is a remarkable person who has lived an extraordinary life. He always was different from the rest of us. He was very serious about our faith and even studied for a long time under Gamaliel in the Sanhedrin."

"Nathan, before we start discussing Paul, let us bow our heads and give God our thanks.

> Dear God, we thank you for this day, for our family and friends, for our health, and for the food which we are about to receive. May your name be praised forever? Amen.

"Tonight, we want to know why you even met with Paul. He had become unclean because of his association with Gentiles and his forsaking our faith. Why did you meet with him?"

"At first, my curiosity got the better of me. I wanted to know why the Jewish leaders tried to kill him and what his side of the story was. I wanted to know why he was in Rome, why he was under house arrest, and why he appealed to the Emperor. I felt I knew him well enough from our childhood and thought there must be some mistake. Samuel, you will remember, Paul always tried to do what was right and proper, and now I thought he had lost his way."

"Yes, I would agree."

"Mary, what is your question?"

"Have Gentile ways corrupted Paul? We are surrounded by them here in Tarsus. We all know how immoral they are. How can Paul proclaim that this new faith is from God? Gentiles create and worship their own gods who make no demands on them and allow them to do whatever they wish. They even have a god they call Bacchus whom they claim is the god of wine and revelry. Maybe that is why they say that this Jesus is God."

"You have some very good questions. I asked similar questions of Paul."

"Well, what did he say about Gentile immorality? Our Law forbids the reckless use of our bodies. Men are supposed to be husbands and fathers, and women are supposed to be wives and mothers. Men and women are forbidden to have common contact with anyone except close family members and friends."

"You are quite right. Paul said the Gentiles' immorality was offensive to him, too. He had reprimanded them and taught them proper behavior."

"Well, how did he do that? I can't imagine Gentiles refraining from doing anything they wanted to do."

"I do not think we Jews have any right to be so sanctimonious. Our past history was similar to and perhaps worse than the Gentiles."

"How can you say that Nathan?"

"Just think back on what the prophets Amos, Hosea, Isaiah, and Jeremiah had to say for God about our drunken ancestors who prostituted themselves with everyone and with foreign powers. Let me give you one of many examples. Do you remember what the prophet Jeremiah said to our people in the early part of his life as a prophet? Speaking for God, he said:

> How can I pardon you? Your children have forsaken me, and have sworn by those who are no gods. When I fed them to the full, they committed adultery and trooped to the houses of harlots. They were well-fed lusty stallions, each neighing for his neighbor's wife. Shall I not punish them for these things? Says the Lord; and shall I not avenge myself on a nation such as this? Go up through her vine-rows and destroy, but make not a full end; strip away her branches, for they are not the Lord's for the house of Israel and the house of Judah have been utterly faithless to me, says the Lord. They have spoken falsely of the Lord, and have said, 'He will do nothing; no evil will come upon us, nor shall we see sword or famine. The prophets are nothing but wind, for the word is not in them. Thus, shall it be done to them.[95]

"Jeremiah spelled out our condition before the Babylonian exile very well. The people gave God no choice with their rampant idolatry and immorality."

"Mary, what did you want to say?"

"We learned, bitterly learned, as a people that we must listen to and obey God's word as given to us through the prophets. But we learned our lesson well. Ever since the exile, we have not deviated from obedience to God and God's word. We did not allow ourselves to be Hellenized by the Greeks. Our men do not do gymnastics naked as the Greeks do. We cover our bodies and keep them holy. Why bring up our past history Nathan?"

"It tells me that our people committed the same crimes as the Gentiles. Our people did not want to be told what to do. But they knew better because of our long history with God. The Gentiles do not know God. Nor do they have a similar history with God. The Gentiles have worshiped silly gods and polluted their lives and their children's lives with their crazy beliefs. Paul told me of a message he gave in their market place to the polytheistic believers of Athens. I wrote it down. Let me get it out. Here it is. Paul said:

> Athenians, I see how extremely religious you are in every way. For as I went through the city and looked carefully at the objects of your worship, I found among them an altar with the inscription, 'To an unknown god.' What therefore you worship as unknown, this I proclaim to you. The God who made the world and everything in it, he who is Lord of heaven and earth, does not live in shrines made by human hands, nor is he served by human hands, as though he needed anything, since he himself gives to all mortals life and breath and all things. From one ancestor he made all nations to inhabit the whole earth, and he allotted the times of their existence and the boundaries of the places where they would live, so that they would search for God and perhaps grope for him and find him—though indeed he is not far from each one of us. For 'In him we live and move and have our being'; as even some of your own poets have said, 'For we too are his offspring.'
>
> Since we are God's offspring, we ought not to think that the deity is like gold, or silver, or stone, an image formed by the art and imagination of mortals. While God has overlooked the times of human ignorance, now he commands all people everywhere to repent, because he has fixed a day on which he will have the world judged in righteousness by a man whom he has appointed, and of this he has given assurance to all by raising him from the dead.[96]

"What do you want to say Rachel?"

"Paul is right. The Greeks should be able to discern God's presence in this world and should not worship anything made with their hands. And the day of the Lord will be a day of jubilation for us and a day of destruction for Gentiles. But what does Paul mean in the last part of his message? Who is this person who has risen from the dead? Surely, he is not talking about Jesus, the carpenter?"

"Yes, he is. Paul and the Christians believe that Jesus will come again and will judge us all on Judgment Day and that this Judgment Day will not be as we Jews believe it will be. What is your question Mary?"

"I think you are getting off the subject. How does Paul teach the Gentiles morality? That is what I want to know."

"All right, Mary, but we will have to return to this subject of Judgment Day before long because it is all part of God's plan."

"God's plan or Paul's plan? I think we know God's plan better than Paul."

"To answer your question Mary, Paul wrote numerous letters that have circulated among the Christian churches that he founded. One such letter was written to the Christians in Corinth. Another letter was sent to Rome while Paul was under house arrest in Caesarea."

"Why was he under arrest? Who arrested him?"

"Do you remember the famine years ago, in the mid-fifties?"

"Yes!"

"Paul took up a collection for starving Christians in Jerusalem. Paul figures he traveled by foot and boat at least 10,000 miles preaching Jesus' message. Wherever he went he asked for a donation to help the starving Christians in Jerusalem to buy food. Food was scarce and prices were higher than most people could pay. The children weren't even playing, because they were starving."

"I remember how we helped the starving Jews in Jerusalem. It was awful."

"Well, Paul brought the money he collected and gave it to the Christian elders, and he told them about his missionary work and the large number of Diaspora Jews and Gentiles that converted to Christianity. The elders rejoiced at God's work through Paul and were grateful to receive the money. But Paul could sense something was the matter. So he asked them what was bothering them."

"And?"

"They told him that many Jews have come to believe that Jesus is the Messiah and the fulfillment of the Law. But they also believe that upholding the Law of Moses is of the utmost importance. They didn't like what Paul was teaching the Gentiles and that it was not necessary to follow the observances set down by Moses. They think that living a good, pure life and following Jesus' message is not enough to be one of Jesus' disciples. These Jewish Christians are bound to hear that you are in Jerusalem. And they are bound to search you out and find you. They don't like you, and they will make trouble for you."

"So the elders devised a plan for him. They asked Paul to join a group of four men who will undergo the ceremony of purification set down by the Jewish Law. They said, 'You will prove to these Jewish Christians that although you say that the Gentiles do not have to obey the Law of Moses, that at least you obey the Law of Moses and that you live your life as a Jewish Christian.'"

"Although Paul was not so sure that what the elders suggested was the best thing to do, he did what the elders suggested. He spent seven days with the four men. For seven days they stayed in the Temple and went through our ceremony of purification. While Paul was in the Temple, many people saw the four other men and they saw Paul with them."

"Now some Jews from a province in Asia, where Paul had done a lot of preaching and teaching about Jesus to Gentiles, saw Paul in the Temple. These Jews immediately jumped to the conclusion that the four men who were with Paul were Gentiles. These four men with Paul were Jewish, not Gentiles. But the Jews from Asia believed that Paul had brought Gentiles into the Temple. They were furious and started shouting angrily."

"Help! An outrage! Men of Israel, this man Paul is in our Temple with Gentiles! Sacrilege! He took these Gentiles past the Sign. NO MAN OF FOREIGN RACE IS TO ENTER WITHIN THESE GATES AND FENCE. IF ANYONE IS TAKEN IN THE ACT, LET HIM KNOW THAT HE HAS HIMSELF TO BLAME FOR THE PENALTY OF DEATH THAT FOLLOWS.[97]

"Paul gets into trouble because of this sign and the belief that the four men with him were Gentiles. An angry crowd immediately gathered and dragged Paul from the Temple. Then they started to beat him. A bystander sought help from the Roman troops to break up the beating. The commander tried to find out what Paul had done. But the mob kept shouting, 'Kill him! Kill him!'"

"So what happened? Surely Paul was innocent. Why did the Romans detain him?"

"I suppose they feared more riots. If Paul were the cause of riots, they needed to know why. In the meantime, they felt he should be kept safely behind bars. Paul tried to explain to the crowd who he was, but they would not listen to him. The tribune tried to beat the cause of the riot out of Paul; but when he learned that Paul was a Roman citizen, he unbound him."

"The next day the Roman tribune took Paul before the Sanhedrin, but the Pharisees and the Sadducees got into a violent fight with each other regarding their beliefs in the resurrection. Fearing for Paul's life, the tribune orders his soldiers to return Paul to prison."[98]

"Then a group of 40 men took an oath to kill Paul. They plotted with the chief priests who were to ask for Paul to appear before them. The men would then intercept Paul in transit before he got to the Sanhedrin and kill him. Paul's nephew overheard the plot. He told Paul about it. Paul had his nephew tell the tribune."

"Was that why Paul was sent to Felix?"

"Yes. In the cover of night and with a heavy guard, Paul was taken to Caesarea. Felix, the Roman governor, kept Paul under house arrest and refused to let Paul stand trial before the Sanhedrin in Jerusalem. What's your question Samuel?"

"But wasn't it Festus who heard his case?"

"Yes, Festus took over after Felix. Festus left Paul in prison in order to please the Temple authorities. They tried to get Festus to turn Paul over to them, but Festus refused. Instead he heard the case and the angry charges made against Paul. When it looked that Paul would be turned over to the chief priests, Paul appealed as a Roman citizen to Caesar. That appeal saved Paul from his enemies, but it also put him at the mercy of Caesar. So Paul was sent to Rome for trial. He was under house arrest in Rome when I met him."

"Mary, what's your question?"

"I still want to hear Paul's teachings on morality."

"Paul wrote several letters to various churches. Copies were made of these letters and were circulated among the churches. While under house arrest in Caesarea, Paul wrote a lengthy letter to the Romans in preparation for his arrival there under Roman guard. He also wrote a letter from Ephesus to a church in Corinth that spells out proper moral and ethical behavior required by the Christian church. Since Paul's letter to the Corinthians is an earlier letter, let me read what I wrote on this parchment from it."

> Do you not know that wrongdoers will not inherit the kingdom of God? Do not be deceived! Fornicators, idolaters, adulterers, male prostitutes, sodomites, thieves, the greedy, drunkards, revilers, robbers—none of these will inherit the kingdom of God. And this is what some of you used to be. But you were washed, you were sanctified, you were justified in the name of the Lord Jesus Christ and in the Spirit of our God...
>
> The body is meant not for fornication but for the Lord, and the Lord for the body. And God raised the Lord and will also raise us by his power. Do you not know that your bodies are members of Christ? Should I therefore take the members of Christ and make them members of a prostitute? Never! Do you not know that whoever is united to a prostitute becomes one body with her? For it is said, "The two shall be one flesh." But anyone united to the Lord becomes one spirit with him. Shun fornication! Every sin that a person commits is outside the body; but the fornicator sins against the body itself. Or do you not know that your body is a temple of the Holy Spirit within you, which you have from God, and that you are not your own? For you were bought with a price; therefore glorify God in your body.[99]

"Rachel and Mary, why are you shaking your heads?"

"Paul says that all these people in this church in Corinth did all these vile things. How can he associate with them? What makes him think they are sanctified or made holy for our God? That's blasphemy. We wouldn't let them in our synagogues."

"I agree. It looks like Paul's fame is that he ministers to the unclean and vile. No wonder our religious leaders wanted to execute Paul."

"Ladies, you are missing the point. These people no longer behave this way. They were baptized. They were washed of their sins and became a part of Jesus' faith community. They are changed people. They have been transformed by the gospel and its healing power. It is as though they were sick and are now made well. Sin no longer has the final word."

"Let it be known that I, Mary, find that kind of thinking hard to take. 'Oh, Paul, I am sorry for my sins. Will you baptize me? Then everything will be right between God and me. And I will go right on sinning.'"

"Mary, once these people are baptized, they are supposed to give up their pagan ways. They are not supposed to sin. Sins of the flesh reveal the desires and sins of the heart and mind. Did you notice how Paul says they were bought with a price?"

"Yes, what did he mean?"

"Jesus redeemed sinners with his blood when he died on the cross. He was the perfect sacrifice. He was spotless like the best lamb we sacrifice on our altars for God to remove our sins from us. God gives even the Gentiles a chance. They did not have our special relationship with God. They did not have our Law to guide them. But Paul says that once they heard the gospel message, they repented just as quickly and as easily as did the people in Nineveh that Jonah was sent to warn. Do you remember Samuel what we were taught?"

"Yes. I remember how Amos pleaded with our ancestors to no avail. He said:

> Seek good, and not evil, that you may live; and so the Lord, the God of hosts, will be with you…Hate evil and love good, and establish justice in the gate; it may be that the Lord, the God of hosts, will be gracious to the remnant of Joseph.[100]

God was willing to forgive the people so that they could have a new start. But they would not listen to God's pleas through his prophet Amos. So God abandoned them to the consequences of their own sins."

"Precisely. Paul wrote along these same lines in his letter to the Romans. I also have a part of this letter and have it with me tonight to explain Paul's beliefs. He writes:

> I am not ashamed of the gospel; it is the power of God for salvation to everyone who has faith, to the Jew first and also to the Greek. For in it the righteousness of God is revealed through faith for faith; as it is written, 'The one who is righteous will live by faith.'
>
> For the wrath of God is revealed from heaven against all ungodliness and wickedness of those who by their wickedness suppress the truth. For what can be known about God is plain to them…So they are without excuse; for though they knew God, they did not honor him as God or give thanks to him, but they became futile in their thinking, and their senseless minds were darkened. Claiming to be wise, they became fools; and they exchanged the glory of the immortal God for images resembling a mortal human being or birds or four-footed animals or reptiles.
>
> Therefore God gave them up in the lusts of their hearts to impurity, to the degrading of their bodies among themselves, because they exchanged the truth about God for a lie and worshiped, and served the creature rather than the Creator, who is blessed forever![101]

"I thought you would appreciate Paul's thoughts. It is getting late. I better be going. I have a long day tomorrow."

"Will you be so kind to join us one more night before you return to Rome?

"Yes, Samuel, I will. But tomorrow night I need to conclude some business before setting sail."

"How will the night after tomorrow be?"

"That will be fine. Thank you all for dinner and conversation. Shalom!"

"Shalom!

***

Thomas: I find the conversations conducted in this video most revealing.

Anita: How so?

Thomas: For one thing, I can understand why the Jewish people of Paul's time felt the way they did towards the Gentile Christians. Recently, I watched the gory and amoral series *Spartacus* on TV that I assume reflected pagan Roman culture even though the events in this historical fiction occurred less than 100 years before the birth of Jesus. Men and women had multiple sexual relations outside of marriage and in the presence of their spouses. It seemed to be the norm of the day, at least for the privileged.

Edward: I also watched a few of those *Spartacus* episodes but found them to be too disgusting. Most offensive was the forced mating of slaves and that their sexual act be performed in front of others for the viewers' entertainment. Also, male slaves had a choice between the arena and the mines. Those men who chose to become a gladiator were trained and then forced to fight each other to the death in the arena with thousands of people cheering the slaughter. Then when a gladiator killed his opponent, the women in the stands bared their breasts.

Thomas: Nothing new there. Such behavior goes on today in movies and on TV. It is almost proscriptive that if movie producers and their writers want to be successful there must be a certain amount of porn, violence, and betrayal. And Christians support this industry? Why don't they walk their talk?

Anita: You two have made an excellent comparison between the first century Gentile culture and today. So do you think Mary's complaint in the video against the Gentiles is justified?

Milton: Before you answer that question, we should do an in-depth study of pagan society for the well born and the masses. We can't let the movie *Spartacus* influence our thinking.

Anita: I suppose you are right Milton. We would need to study the pagan culture of both the masses and the well born. Judging by Paul's letters, we do know that a certain amount of immorality did exist even among the early Gentile Christians.

Sarah: And Mary had every right to object to the inclusion of Gentiles into the Jewish faith community. Their lack of circumcision also shows their ignorance of the Law and the necessity to observe it. Most Jews in the first century lived by a high moral standard such as Samuel and his family. Gentile Christians must not have observed this standard because Paul had to instruct them in the ways of the Law and morality.

Mary: That's true. Paul wrote that "fornicators, idolaters, adulterers, male prostitutes, thieves, the greedy, drunkards, revilers, robbers –none of these will inherit the kingdom of God."[102]

Thomas: O.K. But I don't think the Jewish approach is above reproach when the sign in the Temple warned foreigners not to enter "these gates and fence" otherwise death awaited them. Seems exclusionary to me.

Milton: We live in an exclusionary society. Often we need a ticket to get into some place. We are not allowed unregulated entrance into private homes, clubs, schools, the Statue of Liberty, certain meetings, the White House and Congress, and so on? Population flows need to be controlled. And today, we have to be especially careful with terrorists and mentally ill people inflicting injury on others.

Anita: Wow! You all have raised more questions we individually must consider. For now, we must close this meeting. At our next meeting, we will consider Paul's role in shaping the early church.

Think About It

- Who or what do people worship today? Whom do they serve?
- Why does Paul write that fornicators, idolaters, adulterers, thieves, etc. will not inherit the Kingdom of God?
- Is Paul correct in his understanding?
- How similar or different are your thoughts from Paul's on morality?
- Do you agree with Thomas and Edward on their thoughts on porn and violence today?

Chapter 17

The Emerging Church, Part III

If I speak in the tongues of mortals and of angels, but do not have love, I am a noisy gong or a clanging cymbal... and if I have all faith, so as to remove mountains, but do not have love, I am nothing.

1 Cor. 13:1-3

Anita: Today we will watch the final video segment on Jewish/ Christian cultural and religious understandings regarding the emerging Christian church. It ends with Nathan's final visit with Samuel and his family.

***

"Shalom! Nathan!"

"Shalom! Samuel! Shalom! Rachel! Shalom! Mary."

"Come, let us give thanks to God for the food we are about to receive.

Dear God, we thank you for this opportunity to break bread and to discuss your movement among us. Help us to discern those manifestations that are from you and those that are not

> from you. May this food nourish our bodies and our souls and may we be ever mindful of your blessings. Praise be your name forever. Amen.

I am glad that you could meet with us one more time before you leave for Rome."

"I am happy to be here, too."

"A few nights ago you told us how Paul taught the Gentiles to take proper care of their bodies because now they are a part of the body of Christ."

"We, too, believe we are God's people and therefore need to walk in the ways of the Lord and not expose ourselves or use our bodies immorally. So Mary has a question for you."

"Yes. It seems to me that Paul has taken Jewish religious and moral thinking and applied it to Christianity. Do you agree?"

"Yes, of course. Everywhere Paul went, he first visited our synagogues to preach the gospel message to the Jews. Many Jewish people converted to Christianity, but those conversions make the unconverted Jew that much more hostile toward Paul."

"But why?"

"There are many reasons. Some Jews think Paul is a blasphemer, because he preaches that Jesus is God in the flesh."

"Well, isn't he a blasphemer? Nathan, don't you think he should be put to death according to our Law about blasphemy?"

"I think we need to be careful on this issue. With the advice of Gamaliel, the Sanhedrin did not execute Peter and John when they cured a cripple in the name of Jesus. In fact, Gamaliel warned:

> Fellow Israelites, consider carefully what you propose to do to these men. For some time ago Theudas rose up, claiming to be somebody, and a number of men, about four hundred, joined him; but was killed, and all who followed him were dispersed and disappeared. After him Judas the Galilean

> rose up at the time of the census and got people to follow him; he also perished, and all who followed him were scattered. So in the present case, I tell you, keep away from these men and let them alone; because if this plan or this undertaking is of human origin, it will fail; but if it is of God, you will not be able to overthrow them—in that case you may even be found fighting against God![103]

"Jesus was executed because he claimed he was the Son of God. Maybe he was and maybe he wasn't. We expected a warrior king for a Messiah rather than Isaiah's Suffering Servant. Maybe what the world needs is not another conqueror but someone who will lead us back to our original relationship with God and God's purpose for creating us. It is possible that Jesus was this person who sought to regenerate us spiritually and peacefully."

"Nathan, I think that is a lot of nonsense. We have Moses and the Law to show us the way to God."

"Ah! But has it worked Mary?"

"Yes and no. Many people follow the letter of the Law and do not live out the Spirit of the Law. We all know that. They fool only themselves. God knows what is in their heart. But at least our faith does not permit the lewdness of the Gentiles."

"But Mary, what have we done to show the world God's ways?"

"We welcome Gentiles if they convert to Judaism and observe our Law."

"Do you think that observance of the Law is all that is necessary for our salvation?

"Yes!"

"Well, Paul says that the Law cannot inspire or create faith, that the Law cannot save us. Only through faith will people receive God's Spirit and be saved. The Judaizers, those Jews who have converted to Christianity, disagree with Paul. They believe and try to force Gentile converts to observe the Law and be circumcised. Paul asks those Gentile Christians who think they must obey the Judaizers the following question.

> Does God give you the Spirit and work miracles among you because you do what the Law requires? Or does God give you the Spirit and work miracles among you because you hear the gospel and believe it? Consider the experience of Abraham; as the scripture says, 'He believed God, and because of his faith God accepted him as righteous.' You should realize, then, that the real descendants of Abraham are the people who have faith....Now it is clear that no one is put right with God by means of the Law, because the scripture says, 'Only the person who is put right with God through faith shall live.'[104]

What do you think?"

"That makes sense. Faith is what made Abraham right with God and not the Law. The Law did not even exist then nor was Abraham circumcised at that time. But, we need to hear more."

"You are right Samuel. Let me tell you that Paul has a lot more to say on this subject, and I am not sure I understand it all. I will try to explain to you the best I can. Paul reasons that before Jesus, we were separated from God by our sins. Jesus died as a consequence of them. In other words, our sins were heaped upon Jesus just as we Jews transfer our sins to the sacrificial lamb to bear or take away our sins. Those who believe in Jesus are united with him through their baptism. They are thereby cleansed and released from their sins. Paul says that believers are buried with Jesus in a death like his. Their uniting with him in baptism assures believers in a resurrection like his."

"That's pretty deep theology."

"Well, that is the best I can do. As I told you, Paul traveled over 10,000 miles on his many missionary journeys. In Antioch, he went to the synagogue. After the reading of the Law and the prophets, the rulers of the synagogue asked Paul to speak. So he rose and reviewed our history before introducing what the Sanhedrin and the high priests did to Jesus. Then he said:

> After Jesus died on the cross, they removed him from it, and laid him in a tomb. But God raised him from the dead; and for many days he appeared to his disciples. We bring you the good news that what God promised to the fathers, God has fulfilled to us their children by raising Jesus.
>
> Let it be known to you therefore, brethren, that through Jesus forgiveness of sins is proclaimed to you. Everyone who believes in Jesus and is baptized is set free from all the sins from which the Law of Moses could not set you free.[105]

"As the people were leaving the synagogue, they begged Paul and Barnabas, a missionary traveling with Paul, to return the next Sabbath to continue to explain these things to them. At the next Sabbath, almost the entire city was there to hear Paul speak. But many Jews were filled with jealousy when they saw the multitude. They reviled and contradicted Paul and Barnabas. Paul reacted to these opponents by saying:

> It was necessary that the word of God should be spoken first to you. Since you thrust it from you and judge yourselves unworthy of eternal life, behold, we turn to the Gentiles. For the Lord has commanded us, saying 'I have set you to be a light for the Gentiles, that you may bring salvation to the uttermost parts of the earth.'[106]

"When the Gentiles heard this, they were glad and glorified God. But the Jews stirred up the leading citizens and drove

Paul and Barnabas out of the city. Paul told me that he and Barnabas shook the dust from their feet and went to Iconium. Paul's message in Iconium was much the same. But sitting in the crowd was a man who was crippled from birth. Paul healed him of his infirmity. Immediately the man jumped up and walked."

"Paul, too, can heal people?"

"Oh, yes. He healed many people. But the people in Iconium believed Paul and Barnabas were gods. They thought Paul was Hermes and Barnabas was Zeus. The people rushed to give them garlands and wanted to make sacrifices to them. What are you muttering Rachel?"

"Those people in Iconium must be pretty simple minded to think Paul and Barnabas were Greek gods. I suppose they let the people make them gods?"

"No. They did not. Paul and Barnabas tore their clothes and said:

> Men, why are you doing this? We also are men, of like nature with you, and bring you good news, that you should turn from these vain things to a living God who made the heaven and the earth and the sea and all that is in them.[107]

"But the people would not listen to them. Then some Jews came from Antioch and joined with the Jews of Iconium. They persuaded these people to drag Paul from the city and stone him until he was dead. The crowds thought they had left Paul dead. But when his disciples came to get his body, Paul rose up and entered the city with them. Paul continued to preach in Iconium and Antioch. He established churches in both places."[108]

"I guess it was easier for Paul to establish his churches when the people saw that he survived a stoning?"

"Maybe. I couldn't say for sure. I do know that he suffered a lot. He believed God sent suffering upon him so that he would not become proud. He claims he has a thorn in his side that gives him great discomfort and pain. Paul told me:

> Three times I asked the Lord that this problem leave me. But the Lord answered me: 'My grace is sufficient for you, for my power is made perfect in weakness.' For the sake of Christ, then, I am content with weaknesses, insults, hardships, persecutions, and calamities; for when I am weak, then I am strong.[109]

Samuel?"

"Paul sounds like he has a martyr complex."

"Not really. He truly suffers. He spends all his energy teaching the people about Jesus the Christ, and then some evil manipulators either from within the church or outside the church try to undo his hard work. For instance, many people in the church in Corinth were boastful of their position and knowledge of the faith. They acted as though they had secret knowledge that was given to them only. This knowledge made them proud and boastful. They believed themselves superior to the rest of the congregation."

"These people sound like our scribes and Pharisees."

"Jesus would call these people pious hypocrites."

"What makes people behave like that? Why do people behave as though they are superior to everyone else? Father, can you address that question?"

"I will try. I suppose they have a sense of insecurity. They have unmet needs such as love. Those who love themselves more than they love other people as God's special creation are incapable of true love."

"And they need to feel important."

"Also, many insecure people are ruthless and reckless. They do not care whom they hurt or squash on their way to a superior status. These people grab all they can. But at the root of their behavior is power. They want power. They want power over other peoples' lives. Power forms the basis for most conflicts and struggles in life. Don't you agree Nathan?"

"I agree with what you say. These people created severe division within the church at Corinth. Paul writes to them and admonishes them by describing his life as an apostle. He contrasts and compares his life as an apostle of Jesus Christ to their false illusions of greatness. He says:

> For I think that God has exhibited us apostles as last of all, like men sentenced to death; because we have become a spectacle to the world, to angels and to men. We are fools for Christ's sake, but you are wise in Christ. We are weak, but you are strong. You are held in honor, but we in disrepute. To the present hour we hunger and thirst, we are ill-clad and buffeted and homeless and we labor working with our own hands. When reviled, we bless; when persecuted, we endure; when slandered, we try to conciliate; we have become, and are now, as the scum of the world.[110]

Paul takes a lot of abuse from the Christian converts he has made. He shared with me his idea on peoples' social and religious status. He believes all Christians, great and lowly, Jew and Gentile, slave and free, all belong to Jesus Christ because they are baptized by the same Holy Spirit and the Holy Spirit is one. No person in and of the body of Christ is more important than another person. Paul told me:

> The body does not consist of one member but of many. If the foot should say, 'Because I am not a hand, I do not belong to the body,' that would not make it any less a part of the body. And if the ear should say, 'because I am not an eye, I do not

> belong to the body, each one of them as God chose....All parts of the body are dependent on the other parts of the body.[111]

Paul tells the Corinthians that if they are truly a part of the body of Christ there should be no discord, no feelings of superiority, and no desire to have power over others. He recommends a more excellent way. Then Paul gave me the most wonderful insight on how real love permits us to live peaceably with oneself and with one another. He said that love surpasses any of the other gifts, talents, and feelings of superiority that people have. Love is the great gift of the Spirit. Would you like to hear what he has to say?"

"Yes."

> If I speak in the tongues of men and of angels, but have not love. I am a noisy gong or a clanging cymbal. And if I have prophetic powers, and understand all mysteries and all knowledge, and if I have all faith so as to remove mountains, but have not love, I am nothing. If I give away all I have, and if I deliver my body to be burned, but have not love, I gain nothing.[112]

I really like his thoughts about love."

"I can accept what Paul says about love. But Nathan, tell me what you think drives Paul and these new converts? What is it that makes Christianity both an extension of Judaism and something beyond Judaism?"

"Well, that is a big question. I keep asking myself those questions, too. I already told you about his belief in God in Jesus and the empowerment of believers with God's Spirit. But there is another belief I have not mentioned and that is the Christian belief in the resurrection."

"We Pharisees believe in the resurrection."

"Yes, I know that. But Paul believes that Christians must first believe that Jesus rose from the dead. Again, it is some people in the church of Corinth who deny the possibility of resurrection for Christians. Paul's argument with the Corinthians goes as follows.

> How can you say there is no resurrection from the dead? If there is no resurrection, then Christ did not rise from the dead. If Jesus did not rise from the dead, then my preaching has been misleading and in vain. If Jesus did not rise from the dead, then your faith is in vain and you still have the burden of your sins. Your sins then have not been cancelled by Jesus' death. Those who died with Jesus Christ then are dead and do not have new life.
>
> But I assert that Christ's resurrection establishes a new order. Death entered the world through Adam, the first man. Through Jesus all will be made alive.[113]

You may ask how will the dead have new life through Jesus? How are they raised? What kind of body will the dead have?"

"Good questions. Tell us how."

"Paul makes a comparison to seeds that are sown in one form and after they are sown and begin to grow have another form. These seeds die in order for new life to begin. Then God gives the dead a new form. Paul says that our old body dies, that it is perishable. Our new body, our resurrected body will be like Jesus' resurrected body. Our new body will be a spiritual body and imperishable. Paul says:

> So is it with the resurrection of the dead. What is sown is perishable, what is raised is imperishable. It is sown in dishonor, it is raised in glory. It is sown in weakness, it is raised in power. It is sown a physical body, it is raised a spiritual

> body....I tell you this brethren: flesh and blood cannot inherit the kingdom of God, nor does the perishable inherit the imperishable...Death has lost its sting.[114]

Does that make sense to you?

"Well, I remember Paul was always good at arguing and making his point. But on the resurrection and that Jesus is the key to the resurrection of the body, I cannot accept."

"We agree."

"Our time is quickly running out. Could you tell us where Paul is and what the Emperor's decision was?"

"Yes. Paul knew his days were numbered when he got to Rome. He wrote letters to inspire young people who were continuing his work. In his letters to Timothy, one of his field workers, he writes:

> Fight the good fight of the faith; take hold of the eternal life to which you were called when you made your confession of faith....Command those who are rich in the things of this life not to be proud, but to place their hope, not in such an uncertain thing as riches, but in God...Command them...to be generous and to share with other...
>
> The time will come when people will not listen to sound doctrine, but will follow their own desires and will collect for themselves more and more teachers who will tell them what they are itching to hear...
>
> But you must keep control of yourself in all circumstances; endure suffering, do the work of a preacher of the Good News, and perform your whole duty as a servant of God.[115]

"I heard various stories about what happened to Paul. Some people say that he went to Spain to convert people there. Others say that Nero had his head cut off. I understand he wrote these parting words to Timothy.

> As for me, the hour has come for me to be sacrificed; the time is here for me to leave this life. I have done my best in the race. I have run the full distance, and I have kept the faith. And now there is waiting for me the prize of victory awarded for a righteous life, the prize which the Lord, the righteous Judge, will give me on that Day—and not only to me, but to all those who wait with love for him to appear.[116]

So I think Paul probably died in Rome."

"You know a lot about Paul and his thoughts on God and this Jesus of Nazareth. Have you become a Christian and are you recommending that we become Christians?"

"Not yet. But I am giving my decision careful thought. But for now, I must go. My ship and its cargo are ready to set sail early in the morning. I will write you a letter about my decision.

"Shalom. Thank you for your hospitality."

"Shalom, Nathan. May you have a safe passage to Rome."

***

Sarah: I align myself with Samuel and his family and everything they had to say about Paul. Oh, I have to agree that there were power issues amongst the Jews and Christians of their day just as there are today. Some people use every opportunity at their disposal to promote themselves at the expense of someone else.

Edward: I agree. As I have stated in the past, I reject authoritarian and all-knowing religions that claim to govern people in

God's name. Many of the religious practices during the first century still continue to this day.

Mary: Such as.

Edward: Male supremacy. As you know, many religious organizations such as the Roman Catholic Church will not ordain women as priests. Women are kept in subordinate positions within the church. And Paul helped support this patriarchal agenda.

Mary: I have to agree with you. In 1 Timothy 11-12, Paul writes: "Let a woman learn in silence with full submission. I permit no woman to teach or to have authority over a man; she is to keep silent."

These words have haunted women through the ages and gave men the power to keep women in subservient positions. In the future, I think Roman Catholic women will be ordained as priests. Within the last half century, the Episcopal Church started to ordain women. Then on November 1, 2006, Katherine Jefferts Schori was the first woman priest to serve a nine-year term as the denomination's presiding bishop. This position is the ecclesiastical equivalent to the Church of England's Archbishop of Canterbury.

Edward: Well, you have a point there.

Anita: When I was attending Yale Divinity School in the 1980's, many of my classmates were Roman Catholic women who had high expectations that they would soon be admitted to the priesthood. Several years later, at an alumni meeting, I reconnected with these women. Their hopes had been dashed. Some were working as parish administrators or educators. Some left the Roman Catholic Church and became ordained ministers in Protestant Churches. Many of the women discouraged their sons from becoming priests. Therefore, the United States Roman Catholic Church has a shortage of priests and has to recruit priests from various countries, many of whom can barely speak English.

Edward: I was unaware of those dynamics. They only reinforce my objections to unchallenged religious authoritarian rule.

Milton: Also, may I add that many Protestant churches are reluctant to call women as their senior ministers.

Anita: We could go on about power issues that definitely exist; but with the time left to us, I want us to reflect on Paul's letters to Timothy that outline what Christian discipleship should be about. Why does Paul write that we must fight the good fight of the faith, not to be proud, and to rely only on God and not on riches?

Mary: I suppose there is always someone or something or challenge that can consume our time, energy, and thought that causes us to forget about God and God's will and our part in God's kingdom.

Anita: Well said. How does this busyness affect our souls and those of our children?

Thomas: I am a perfect example of a person who grew up without any thought of God. My parents should have at least given me a religious foundation within either the Christian or Jewish faith. Instead, other people and I have explored various religions, many of which are self-centered, self-serving, and offer no spiritual value to me and the wider world. Ignorance and false teachings are not blest.

Sarah: Since Christianity grew out of Judaism, my daughter and her husband have agreed to educate and raise their children as Jews and as Christians. At least this way, their children will have a sound religious foundation.

Milton: That's an enlightened approach to teaching children about God. At least they will have an educated religious foundation to guide them on their spiritual journey. Congratulate them.

Anita: Paul warns us of a danger we can encounter when we are not taught and fail to adhere to sound doctrine. He says:

> For the time is coming when people will not put up with sound doctrine, but having itching ears, they will accumulate for themselves teachers to suit their own desires, and will turn away from listening to the truth and wander away to myths.[117]

Thomas: Isn't that what New Age religion is all about? They make up their own set of beliefs, their own reality, and have discovered their own "divinity" within themselves. I know. I tried it all such as meditation, crystals, Buddhism, breathing exercises, channeling, and so on. Even the medical profession buys into some of this Have-It-Your Way religion when their treatment fails. So they put the burden for healing on the person. It is all a subtle deception.

Anita: Wow! Thomas, you surprise me. I have never connected New Age religion with Paul's warnings. I think your insight is correct. I know of some churches that unwittingly let certain church members bring in the teachings and representatives of New Age and Eastern religions into their meditation groups. All such behavior is far from sound Christian teachings.

Sarah: I never gave New Age religion any thought. But Thomas you have raised the red flag for danger ahead within our synagogues as well. Of course, cults can also fall into this category of wandering from the truth into myths. They also create psychological and spiritual havoc for the innocent and vulnerable person seeking illumination about God. I appreciate your sharing your thoughts with us.

Anita: I am amazed with today's discussion. We will have to return to it in more depth when we start a new series on Trinitarian and Atonement theology. We have only one more meeting before we break for the summer. At our final meeting, we will discuss the spread of Christianity and persecution.

Think About It

- Despite all kinds of hardships and a near death experience, why do you suppose Paul continued in his work?
- Paul believes it is faith alone in Jesus that saves people. Why do you think Paul believed this way?
- Do you agree with the people in the video that power issues are the basis for all conflict? What makes you think so?
- Do you agree with what the first few lines of 1 Corinthians 13 says regarding love?
- Have you ever known a loveless Christian?
- Is such a person a Christian?
- Do you believe that a religion based on what we want to hear rather than what we should hear is not from God and is a form of idolatry? What makes you think so?

Chapter 18

The Spread of Christianity and Persecutions

The resurrection of Jesus Christ is our hope today. It is our assurance that we have a living Savior to help us live as we should now, and that when, in the end, we set forth on that last great journey, we shall not travel an uncharted course, but rather we shall go on a planned voyage—life to death to eternal life.

Queens' Gardens
Raymond MacKendree

Anita: Christianity is born out of the Jewish faith and considers itself the new Israel. In the beginning of the Christian movement, Rome considered it to be a sect of Judaism and therefore a legal religion.

Milton: Rome did not grant new religions legal status. As long as Christianity is considered a sect of Judaism, Rome grants the Jewish religious leaders the authority to persecute and prosecute Christians. Sometime around 100 CE, Christians are officially excommunicated from the synagogues and lose their status and protection as a "legal religion" within the Roman Empire.

Anita: Temple authorities, Pharisees, Sadducees, priests, and scribes cooperate with the Romans in keeping the peace. They feared Rome's power yet learned to use it to their own advantage.

Milton: Two sects within the Jewish community that the Jewish leaders were unable to control are the Zealots and the Christians. The Zealots are the super nationalists who believed that the only solution to Roman rule was to overthrow it.

Anita: Roman procurators assigned to Israel, in the second half of the first century, are insensitive to the Jewish people and their faith. These Roman procurators are more in sympathy with the non-Jews living in Israel than with the Jews.

Milton: About 50 CE, a Roman soldier, stationed in front of the Temple, makes an obscene gesture that infuriates the Jewish people. They demand the Roman soldier be punished for blasphemy. The Jews start to stone him. The Roman troops rush in to restore order. Panic follows and many people are trampled to death.

Civil war between various Jewish factions and between Jews and Gentiles engulfs Israel. The Jewish historian Josephus gives detailed accounts of what happened during these times in *The Wars of the Jews.*

Anita: Yes, Josephus is an excellent source for what happened during this period of history. In 66 CE, Eleazar, the son of Ananias the High Priest, conspires with certain priests to suspend the twice daily sacrifices for the Roman Emperor that were made in the Temple. Many Temple leaders fear retaliation and a serious break in their working relationship with the Romans. They try to reason with these rebels and the danger this action posed for the people of Jerusalem. They seek help from Florus, Rome's procurator.

Sarah: He did nothing because he desired to kindle a war against the Jews. However, King Agrippa sends some 3,000 soldiers who fail to subdue the rebellion. The rebels force his soldiers to retreat from the Temple area. Then the rebels burn the home of the High Priest, the palace of King Agrippa, and the archives that hold their records of indebtedness.

Thomas: Smart way to get rid of debt slavery.

Sarah: Inside Jerusalem, power struggles occur among the various militant groups. No group thinks the leader of the opposing group worthy of their loyalty. Each group slays large numbers of the opposing groups. The victors attack the Roman soldiers caught inside the Jerusalem walls. These soldiers offer to surrender their weapons if no harm will come to them. Eleazar's men agree. The Romans lay down their arms. Then Eleazar's men slay the Roman soldiers.

Outside Jerusalem, Gentiles and Jews fight each other. In Caesarea, Gentiles slay 20,000 Jews. Josephus writes of those killed in Syria.

> Greediness of gain was a provocation to kill the opposite party...they without fear plundered the effects of the slain and carried off the spoils of those whom they slew...It was then common to see cities filled with dead bodies, still lying unburied, and those of old men, mixed with infants, all dead, and scattered about together...you might then see the whole province full of inexpressible calamites, while the dread of still more barbarous practices which were threatened, was everywhere greater than what had been already perpetrated.[118]

In Scythopolis, 13,000 more Jews are slaughtered by Gentiles. Violence causes more violence on all sides until the Zealots draw the entire country into war.

Mary: Today's Syrians are suffering similar strife. The war horrors, deaths, and starvation that drive millions from their homes in war-torn countries makes you want to cry. Women and children suffer the most.

Milton: Yes. Violence only begets more violence. The Jewish rebels decimate Rome's 12th Legion. Success is short-lived however. Roman General Vespasian retakes area after area until all of Israel is conquered except for Jerusalem. Nero dies in 68 CE and Vespasian leaves Israel to become Emperor. His son, Titus, lays siege to the walled city of Jerusalem.

Sarah: The Jewish people in Jerusalem suffer greatly. There is no escape, and the radical actions of the Zealots bring suffering onto the entire population. Starvation afflicts all. Zealots go so far as to extract food from people's mouths. Even cannibalism becomes prevalent.

Jewish atrocities toward their own people increase as starvation grows worse. Cadavers are left unburied. Zealots walk over corpses as though they are pebbles. In time, Titus and his men make battering rams to break down the three walls surrounding Jerusalem. Defeat comes in 70 CE. Titus burns the Jerusalem Temple and destroys the city.

Before the Romans take Jerusalem, some 960 Zealots escape to Masada and capture a Roman fortress built by Herod which stands some 1500 feet on a high hilltop above the Dead Sea. Zealots attack and take this fortress. They slaughter the Roman soldiers and seize the armaments stored there. Masada's strategic advantage of height enables the Zealots to keep the Romans from conquering them for three years.

With Jewish slave labor, Titus builds a ramp the height of Masada. A battering ram is pushed up the ramp. Its purpose is to break down the massive doors to the fortress. The night before the Roman offensive of May 2, 73, every single person inside the fortress dies. Suicide is a great sin in the Jewish religion. The Zealots used little pebbles with names on them. These pebbles served as a lottery. The person picked had to kill another person and fathers killed their children and wives. Only one person committed suicide, the last one.

Anita: We learn from Eusebius the cost of the war to the Jewish people. He writes:

> In computing the whole number of those who lost their lives...famine and the sword destroyed 1,100,000 persons; that those who had taken part in sedition and terrorism informed against each other after the capture of the city and were put to death; that the tallest and handsomest of the youngsters were kept for the triumphal procession [in Rome]; that of the rest, those over seventeen were put in irons and sent to hard labor in Egypt, and still more were distributed among the provinces to perish in the theatres by sword or by wild beast, while those under seventeen were carried off captive and sold, the number of these alone reaching 90,000.[119]

The prophets and Jesus had warned that such a world shattering event would occur. But no one heeded their warnings.[120] Literature, known as apocalyptic literature, appears in the Bible. It tells us about the end times for one age and the beginning of a new age. Mark, Luke, and Matthew all write after the fact about these end times. For example, Mark writes that Jesus said:

- The Temple will be destroyed.
- Wars, earthquakes, and famine will all come to past.

- The spread of the gospel will occur.
- Persecutions against Christians will occur, but the Holy Spirit will be with Jesus' disciples.
- False Christs and prophets will lead the people astray.
- Jesus will return to judge everyone and to vindicate the righteous.
- Be alert and watchful.
- The purpose of Jesus' words is to encourage and sustain his disciples in times of tribulations.
- He urges caution and wisdom.

Many Jews and Jewish Christians escape and survive the devastation and destruction of Jerusalem and remain free in the provinces. With the destruction of the Temple, the priestly class becomes unemployed. The Pharisees then become the principal religious leaders of the Jewish people. They gather in Jamnia in 90 CE and decide which of their sacred books should form the canon of Jewish Scripture. Prayers and forms of worship are revised to meet their new situation. Ritual curses against Christians are added to their prayers. Christian scripture is judged heretical and cursed by them. Shortly thereafter, Christians are officially excommunicated from the synagogues and lose their status as a "legal religion" by the Romans.

Christians, too, regroup for the future. Jesus' followers believe that Jesus will return before they die. When Jesus does not return as hoped for, Christians rethink Jesus' words. A follower of Peter gives an answer to the end times and Jesus' Second Coming. He writes:

> But do not ignore this one fact, beloved, that with the Lord one day is as a thousand years, and a thousand years as one day. The Lord is not slow about his promise as some count

slowness, but is forbearing toward you, not wishing that any should perish, but that all should reach repentance.[121]

Milton: Paul holds a different belief. He believes that the end times have already begun with the resurrection of Jesus and with the new life Christians find in Jesus. The writer of the fourth gospel, the Gospel of John, takes the same position.

After the death of James, the brother of Jesus, and shortly before the destruction of Jerusalem, Jewish Christians from Jerusalem seem to lose their prominence in the emerging Christian Church. From that time onward, church leadership develops within the Gentile Christian population in various parts of the Mediterranean.

Anita: The Christian message spreads throughout this world through a common language, Greek. Christian leaders take care to explain the faith intelligently and thoughtfully and through their written documents. In the first century, they preach where large crowds gather, where people can listen, question, and cross-examine them.

Now as promised, we will conclude our study with Nathan's letter to his friend Samuel in Tarsus.

Milton: Before we get into Nathan's letter, let me tell you briefly about the Jewish war against the Romans fought between 132-136 CE. Simon bar Kokhba, whom many Jews regarded as their Messiah, led a large-scale guerrilla force that initially succeeded in overwhelming Roman legions numbering close to 100,000. Bar Kokhba killed Christian Jews when they refused to join him. Emperor Hadrian put this revolt down by amassing and sending one third of Rome's entire army to Israel to defeat and destroy the Jews. About 200,000 to 400,000 Jewish militia were killed with a total of about 580,000 Jews killed by sword, famine, and disease. Most of the remaining population were sold into slavery. Another Jewish revolt was from 351-352. Rome imposed heavy retribution against the Jews and tried to obliterate their religion through genocide and to erase the memory of their existence by renaming Jerusalem to Aelia Capitolina and Israel to Syria Palaestina.

Sarah: I never connected these Jewish wars with anti-Semitism among non-Jews. But they could be the source of such prejudice. I will need to look into the cause and the aftermath of these wars.

Anita: Thank you Milton for giving us this information. Sarah, you have made an important connection to the root cause of anti-Semitism which I never considered.

But for now and before we undertake an entirely new study of Trinitarian and Atonement theology, let us conclude with Nathan's letter.

***

Rome, October 80 CE

Dear Samuel, Rachel, and Mary,

My ship and I arrived safely last month in the evening with Rome's Ostia light house as our guide into port. We had clear skies and strong winds for a large part of our voyage. But with the aid of my newly purchased pelorus (a primitive compass), celestial navigation, Roman light houses and my charts, we sailed the course safely to our destination.

This voyage gave me a lot of time to reflect on the horrors of our Jewish civil wars and the destruction of our faith world, our people and way of life. In a very short time everything disintegrated and went up in smoke because the Zealots used events as an excuse for revolt. The various Zealot groups were only seeking power for themselves and not for the welfare of our people.

So in answer to your parting question whether I have become a Christian and am recommending that you become a Christian, here is my answer.

Christians are peace loving, not only among themselves, but towards others. They have been and continue to be victims of Jewish hostilities. Now that Christianity has spread throughout the Roman world, Nero (d. 68 CE) and others make them their scapegoats for everything. The future does not look good for Christians. Persecutions no doubt will increase from all sides.

But, as you know, Paul was always genuine and trustworthy even though he was initially over-zealous against Christians. I believe that Jesus stopped him on the road to Damascus and recruited him to carry on Jesus' work. Paul had to have had this encounter to change the course of his life. He is humble now and when he was free, he lived in poverty and worked for his own bread while preaching the gospel everywhere. So I believe him. He seeks nothing for himself.

Stoning and killing are not the Christian way. Repentance, forgiveness, love, and self-giving are. Their pathway is not one of revolt and killing of enemies but love for their enemies. I am intrigued with the way they care for the needy, each other, and do not fight back.

I recently bought copies of their Gospels according to Mark and Matthew which became available in 65 and 70 CE respectively. I understand a person named Luke is completing his version of Jesus' life. You should try to get a copy of each gospel for a fuller understanding of who Jesus is. These gospels, Paul, and his letters have convinced me to become a Christian.

You know I am a risk taker with my ships. But with my navigational equipment and charts and responding to changing weather conditions, I have made my livelihood carrying cargo to different parts of the world. I have learned to trust these navigational aids to bring me safely to my destinations. I trust what Paul shared with me and what I have learned about Jesus in the gospels. What troubles me are those men who hijack this new faith to manipulate it to their advantage. They lead people astray as did our religious leaders. They fabricate lies and write fantasy gospels about the life of Jesus. Nevertheless, I intend to be baptized into this faith community next month and pray that the Holy Spirit will be my guide.

I know I am taking a big risk. But that has been the story of my life. I believe God has led me to this decision. I will continue to grow in the Christian faith and rely on the gospels, Paul's letters, and the guidance of the Holy Spirit. They will be my navigational aids and my North Star and reference point for life and for reaching my final destination to dwell in God's presence.

Shalom to all of you,
Nathan

Think About It

- Do you think Nathan's decision is wise? What makes you think so?
- Were you aware of the wars surrounding the destruction of Jerusalem and Israel?
- What lessons can we learn from them?

Epilogue

Choices

Many people let their busy lives consume all their time. They fail to take time out to ask eternal questions and seek enlightenment from God. I have tried to give you messages from God as they are revealed to us in Jesus. Through Jesus' teachings, healings, miracles, parables, suffering, death, and resurrection, our incomprehensible God partially reveals God's self to us. Christians believe that Jesus lived, died on a cross, and rose from the dead. He bled like a man and died like one. And then he was seen and experienced by hundreds of people after his resurrection and before his ascension. He is present to believers today through the Holy Spirit.

To be or not to be a Christian is the question.

In Oscar Wilde's book *The Picture of Dorian Gray,* Dorian elects a pathway in life many people choose to take without realizing the consequences. Dorian Gray is a handsome young man whose portrait is painted by Basil Hallward who is bewitched with Dorian's beauty. While Dorian sits for his portrait, he listens to Lord Henry Wotton expound on his hedonistic and libertine world view and sensual and evil conquests. Lord Henry's lifestyle seduces Dorian. He makes a wish that his portrait will age instead of himself. As Dorian indulges in every sin and vice, his portrait illustrates the ugly tarnish growing on his soul but not on the ageless beauty of his physical person. In old age, Dorian decides to experiment with moral reformation. To see what his latest behavior has done to his portrait, he goes to the sealed room in which his portrait is kept. Instead of a handsome young man, the subject of the portrait is uglier than ever. In his anger that he has not been absolved of his sins, he takes a knife and stabs the portrait. When Dorian stabs it, the servants and people on the street hear his cry. The police are called in. They find an old disfigured man with a knife in his heart and the portrait of the young Dorian next to him on the floor. No one knows who this ugly, evil-looking old man is. Then the servants notice their master's rings on his fingers.

This story of Dorian Gray reminds me of Jesus' parable regarding an empty house. He says:

> When the unclean spirit has gone out of a person, it wanders through waterless regions looking for a resting place, but not finding any, it says, 'I will return to my house from which I came.' When it comes, it finds it swept and put in order. Then it goes and brings seven other spirits more evil than itself, and they enter and live there; and the last state of that person is worse than the first.[122]

In effect, Jesus says that our soul is like an empty house. What fills it matters. Similar to the disintegration of Dorian's soul as illustrated in his portrait before his death, his empty soul became possessed by unholy, evil spirits.

It is not easy to be good and a Christian. Many people reject Christianity because their faith never matured or they were never introduced to it properly. Too often unworthy individuals label themselves as Christian and claim their voice represents the will of

God. Take for example the leaders of the Crusades, the Inquisition, and today's cults. These unworthy leaders did not and do not want to step down from playing God. But thinking Christians know God has a different voice. Through Jesus and the prophets before him, we learn that God is a God of love and peace who seeks to find the lost sheep and redeem the prodigal son. God's relationship with us did not end with Jesus' resurrection. It is open-ended and plays out in our daily lives of love and service or lack thereof. Through Jesus, God liberates us from the powers of evil in society and in our hearts. Evil does not have the last word.

Readiness for life challenges all people. Let me draw upon a lesson I learned from my life on the water. It has taught me that I must be prepared for gale force winds and the 10-20 foot waves that can swamp a boat. To survive, you need to develop sailing skills, have a properly fitted-out boat including navigational equipment, and know when and how to take certain actions based on weather conditions. Many times my husband and I had to seek shelter in some unknown cove. Even then our anchor, line, and tackle had to be strong enough to weather the storm.

Skippers who failed to prepare for bad weather had their boats break free from their moorings and/or anchor. The wind and current would then drive these boats onto the rocks or across large bodies of water to their destruction.

Jesus teaches us to pray "thy kingdom come, thy will be done on earth as it is in heaven." We are meant to walk humbly in the ways of the Lord. We are called to help the vulnerable and be God's hands, voice, heart, and instruments of peace and love in this world.

We, as God's children, are invited to accept God's call to love and serve according to our capacity and gifts. We need to grow in the faith and decide whom we will serve and feed. Know that if the world would embrace Jesus' teachings and make him Lord of their lives, we would all live in peace.

For now, let me conclude with two parting thoughts.

My first thought comes from Psalm 24.

> The earth is the Lord's and all that is in it,
> The world, and those who live in it;
> For he has founded it on the seas and established it on the rivers.
> Who shall ascend the hill of the Lord?
> And who shall stand in his holy place?
> Those who have clean hands and pure hearts,
> Who do not lift up their souls to what is false, and do not swear deceitfully.
> They will receive blessing from the Lord.

My second thought comes from the wisdom of an old Cherokee to his grandson about the battle that goes on inside people.

> He said, "My son, the battle is between two wolves inside us all.
> One is Evil. It is envy, jealousy, greed, arrogance, lies, false pride, ego....
> The other is Good. It is honesty, peace, love, humility, kindness, compassion, faith....
> The grandson thought about it for a minute and then asked his grandfather:
> "Which wolf wins?"
> The old Cherokee replied, "The one you feed."

Glossary

Adoptionists/Ebionites: Early Jewish Christians known as Judaizers who required Gentile converts to live as Jews, to observe the Jewish law, and for the men, to undergo circumcision. They believed that Jesus was human and not divine. He became the Son of God or was adopted at his baptism. See Chapter 8 in *Resurrection Dialogues.*

Annunciation: Gabriel's visit to Mary.

Antichrist: A person who poses as Christ and is a leader of evil forces that possess deceptive powers and lead people away from God.

Apocalyptic: The revelation of hidden things during times of persecution and oppression. This literary genre uses symbolism to hide the true meaning of what is said from the uninitiated. Writers of apocalyptic literature believe that God will bring a catastrophic end to evil and will usher in a new era. Apocalyptic literature encourages people to stand fast; it states that God is in control and will ultimately rescue them.

Apostles: The name given to the twelve men chosen to form Jesus' inner circle.

Canon: The sacred books that form Jewish and Christian holy scripture selected by an authorized council that have set them apart from other religious books. These selected works became the standard or norm and source of authority for a religious community.

Christ: The Greek form of the word *Messiah.*

Darkness: A state of unbelief as well as total evil that cannot overcome the Word.

Devil or Satan: These names refer to evil personified and a person or will that is actively hostile to God.

Disciple: The name given to those followers of Jesus who were not in Jesus' inner circle. They continued to live normal lives; they did not give up everything to follow Jesus around the countryside. Today, people who believe Jesus is the Messiah and live their lives according to Jesus' teachings are considered Jesus' disciples.

Docetists/Marcionites: Early Christians who followed the teachings of Marcion (100-160) who was a polytheist who hated Jews and believed Jesus came from a superior, loving God, not from the Jewish God known as Yahweh. He taught that Jesus was a divine being and not a flesh and blood human. Therefore, Jesus never suffered on the cross. See Chapter 8 in *Resurrection Dialogues.*

Dualistic Views: The view that the material is evil and the spiritual good.

Ebionites: See Adoptionists.

Elect: A belief God chooses some people in preference over others.

God's Will: Christians believe God's will is unity, peace, wholeness, joy, goodness, righteousness, purity, fidelity, love, hope, faithfulness, self-giving and the like.

God's Wrath: God's wrath is not fire bolts reigning down upon us. God's wrath is God's divine reaction to evil. It is God's steadfast and holy hatred of sin.

Good News: The message Jesus proclaims as well as the content of his ministry. Gospel is another name for good news.

Gospel: See above.

Holy Spirit: The Holy Spirit is God's invisible presence with us.

Kingdom of God/Kingdom of Heaven: This Kingdom is a spiritual kingdom where God's universal rule reigns. Everyone will acknowledge God's reign, and a new era of righteousness and peace will begin. It brings with it a transformation of society as well as of the individual. There is a reordering of people's lives in their relation to one another and to God.

Life: Refers to the authentic existence God wants us to have.

Light: The divine illumination of a person's mind and conscience.

Marcionites: See Docetists.

Martyr: "A person who chooses to suffer or die rather than give up his or her faith or principles." (*Webster's Dictionary)*

Messiah: The name given for God's anointed. The Messiah is the deliverer, long awaited by the Jews, who is to restore the fortunes of Israel and usher in a golden age of peace and righteousness. At the time of Jesus' birth, the Jewish people were ruled by the Roman Empire. The Jews expected a glorious warrior-king like King David, who would rescue them. They did not expect their Messiah to be of humble origins born to a peasant woman. In the broadest sense of the word, the Messiah was to work out God's purposes in this world. The Greek form of the word Messiah is Christ.

Miracles: Events that come about through the direct intervention by God in the working of the world. Miracles are difficult for people to understand; they contradict known natural law. Christians believe that the miracles Jesus performed were caused by God working through Jesus.

Number 40: The number used in the Bible to signify a long time and not literally 40 days.

Overshadow: Miraculous circumstances of Jesus' conception and removes any thoughts of any sexual intercourse. The emphasis here is that Jesus has human and divine origins.

Parables: They are open-ended earthly stories that indirectly teach a spiritual truth.

Pharisees: A Jewish faith community which believed in the immortality of the soul, in the resurrection of the body, and in the existence of spirits. They believed that people were rewarded or punished in their future life according to how they lived on earth. They emphasized that religion must be consistent with the Law, and that God's grace was bestowed only on the doers of the Law. Religion became external—what went on in the heart was less important to the Pharisees than outward observance.

Prodigal: An adjective that describes a lavish and wasteful life style.

Proselytes: Non-Jewish people who went through a process of becoming a Jew. Their initiation into the Jewish faith community was through baptism.

Resurrection: A Pharisaic and Christian belief that the dead will rise from death to new life. The rising from the dead of Jesus Christ by the power of God. Jesus' body was transformed into a higher form of life, but he still maintained the same personal presence and activity he had before his crucifixion. Through Jesus' victory over death, Christians believe they will be resurrected and share a new form of existence in spiritual fellowship with God.

Repent/Repentance: *Sorrow* for wrongs we have committed, *an admission of fault,* a *resolve* to live a better life, and an *attempt* to right the wrongs committed. True repentance brings us into a new and better relationship with God.

Satan: See Devil.

Sanctify: Make holy, to set apart as holy, to consecrate.

Scapegoating: The belief that people's sins are removed and transferred to unblemished animals which are killed or cast out into the wilderness. From this practice, we get the psychological and sociological concept.

Sadducees: A Jewish sect which opposed the Pharisees. They were comparatively very few in number, but they were educated men—mostly wealthy and in good positions. Sadducees denied the resurrection of the body, and they held only to the first five books of the Bible. They comprised a priestly and aristocratic people who were out of touch with the ordinary people and with God.

Son of God: A term that has many interpretations. For Jews, it meant a person in a close relationship with God with a divine or specific task. In the New Testament it was used to designate Jesus' unique authority and status in relationship to God.

Right hand of God: A place of honor.

Word: Jesus is part of the power of God that creates and gives life and light. He existed before time and before the creation of the universe.

Endnotes

Chapter 2

[1] Luke 1:35.
[2] Luke 1:38.
[3] See Glossary
[4] See Glossary
[5] Luke 1:46-55.
[6] Matt. 1:21.
[7] Luke 1:46-55.
[8] Num. 18:15-16.
[9] Luke 2:25-28.
[10] Luke 2:36-38.
[11] Matt. 2:2.
[12] Matt. 2:11.

Chapter 3

[13] An adaptation of Luke 3:7.
[14] Dietrich Bonhoeffer, *The Cost of Discipleship* (New York, Collier Books, 1963), 45, 47.
[15] John 1:27.

Chapter 4

[16] Matt. 4:3.

Chapter 5

[17] Matt. 4:5.
[18] Mark 3:22
[19] Mark 9:34, Lk. 22:24.
[20] Matt. 16:24-26.
[21] Matt. 11:28-30.
[22] Mark 1:21-28, Luke 4:31-17.

[23] Luke 4:18-19.
[24] Luke 4:21.
[25] Luke 4:30.
[26] Prov. 8:25, 27, 29-30.

Chapter 6
[27] Mark 2:1-12
[28] Mark 2:5
[29] Mark 2:27
[30] Mark 8:2
[31] John 11:47-53

Chapter 7
[32] Matt. 13:24-30.
[33] Matt. 13:37-40.
[34] Matt. 13:44.
[35] Luke 10:25-37.
[36] Luke 10:27.
[37] Luke 10:25-37.

Chapter 8
[38] Deut. 15:7-11.
[39] Luke 18:9-14.
[40] Luke 15:3:6b-7.
[41] Luke 15:11-23.
[42] Luke 15:29-32.

Chapter 9
[43] Luke 13:31-34.
[44] Mark 8:27-30.
[45] Mark 8:31-33.
[46] Luke 19:42-44.
[47] Zech. 9:9.
[48] Mark 11:17.
[49] Mark 12:38-40.
[50] Mark 12:1-10.
[51] Isa. 5:1-7.

Chapter 10
[52] John 12:1-17.
[53] Mark 14:18-21.
[54] Mark 14:43-50.
[55] Mark 14:62.

[56] Mark 14:64b-65.
[57] John 19:30; Luke 23:46

Chapter 11
[58] Mk 15:31b-32.
[59] Luke 23:34.
[60] Simon Wiesenthal, *The Sunflower, On the Possibilities and Limits of Forgiveness* (New York: Schocken Books, 1997), 54.
[61] See Chapter 3.
[62] Anita Keire, *Resurrection Dialogues with Skeptics and Believers,* (Greenwich, CT: Curriculum Development Associations, Inc., 2015), 164-7.
[63] Dietrich Bonhoffer, *The Cost of Discipleship* (New York, Collier Books, 1963), 48.
[64] Anita Keire, *A Parent's Guide to Prayer* (Old Saybrook, Curriculum Development Associates, Inc., 1992), 42-43.

Chapter 13
[65] Luke 23:34.
[66] Luke 23:43.
[67] John 19:26-27.
[68] Mark 15:34.
[69] John 19:28.
[70] Jn. 19:30.
[71] Lk. 23:46
[72] I have lost the exact reference.
[73] Viktor E. Frankl, *Man's Search for Meaning* (Beacon Press, Boston, 2006), 76-77. Frankl's first edition appeared in German in 1946.
[74] John 19:34.
[75] Mt. 27:63-66.

Chapter 14
[76] Most of the information to follow comes from Luke 24.
[77] Luke 24:13-27.
[78] Isa. 52:13-15.
[79] Isa. 53:1-3.
[80] Isa. 53:4-5.
[81] Luke 24:45-49.
[82] Matt. 28:11-15.
[83] Acts 2:2-4.
[84] Acts 2:38-39.
[85] Acts 3:6.
[86] Acts 5:33-39.

Chapter 15

[87] Acts 7:55-56.

[88] Acts 7 & 8.

[89] Acts 8:1-4.

[90] Acts 9:3-6.

[91] Acts 9:10-19.

[92] Gal. 1 & 2.

[93] Dtr. 6:4-5.

[94] Col. 1:15-20.

Chapter 16

[95] Jer. 5:7-13.

[96] Acts 17:22-31.

[97] William Barclay, *The Acts of the Apostles* (The Westminster Press, Philadelphia, 1955), 171-172.

[98] Acts 23:8-10.

[99] 1 Cor. 6:9-20.

[100] Amos 5:14-15.

[101] Rom. 1:16-25.

[102] 1 Cor. 6:9-20.

Chapter 17

[103] Acts 5:35-39.

[104] Gal. 3:5-11.

[105] Adaptation from Acts 13:16-39.

[106] Acts 13:46-47.

[107] Acts 14:15.

[108] Acts 14:19-23.

[109] 2 Cor. 13:8-10.

[110] 1 Cor. 4:9-13.

[111] 1 Cor. 12:14-31.

[112] 1 Cor. 13:1-3.

[113] Summary of 1 Cor. 15:12-28.

[114] I Cor. 15:42-55.

[115] 1 & 2 Timothy.

[116] 2 Tim. 4:6-8.

[117] 2 Tim. 4:3-4.

Chapter 18

[118] Josephus, *The Works of Josephus* (Hendrickson Publishers, Peabody, 1992), Book 2, Chapter 15.

[119] Eusebius, *The History of the Church from Christ to Constantine* (Dorset Press, Middlesex, UK, 1965), 117.
[120] Isa. 24:1, 4-6, Jer. 4:23-27, Mk. 13.
[121] 2 Pet. 3:8-9.

Epilogue
[122] Luke 11:24-26.

CPSIA information can be obtained
at www.ICGtesting.com
Printed in the USA
BVOW05s0308191216
471213BV00022B/542/P